ISBN   979-8-9883456-1-9   *e-book*
       979-8-9883456-2-6   *hardcover*
       979-8-9883456-3-3   *paperback*

HOW TO BE SECOND

Being Second is a destination, not a stepping stone

NATHAN YOUNG & DAVID HARTMAN, Ph.D.

CONTENTS

HOW TO READ THIS BOOK

WE BELIEVE THAT EVERYTHING we've written here is useful, but depending on who you are and what you're interested in (or struggling with), different sections of this book may be especially useful right away. Here's a quick reference to help you find what you might be looking for.

If you're a First in Command/CEO/Visionary...

If you're interested in how a Second could help you, or you're already partnered with someone like that and you'd like to understand them better, we included a "Summary for First in Commands" section just for you. But if you skip right to the summary, you probably won't understand the words we use. It's a lot of "inside baseball," y'know? So, here's the path we recommend:

1. Read the chapter outline,
2. Read the definition of terms,
3. Read "Summary for First in Commands".

If you're a Second/Integrator/COO...

You know better than we do exactly what you're looking for, and we trust you'll be able to self-guide your way to exactly what you need from this content.

However, if we can make a recommendation, we really have done what we can to craft the book into a journey specifically for you. So, for anyone who would say to themselves, "I think this book is for me," we think that reading the whole book from start to finish will bring you the most joy.

If you're a significant other trying to understand your partner...

We've talked with many partners of Seconds, and digging into the personality traits we've identified has been super helpful for their relationships. Something to the tune of, "they feel like I finally understand them" has landed in our inboxes more than once.

We recommend starting your journey with us by reading the definition of terms, then move to "What is a Second" and "There's Two!" From there, you'll be the best person to choose the next steps of your adventure.

If you're not sure...

Just dig in. You might find yourself in these pages, or maybe you won't. Remember, if you're a Second, that's wonderful! If you're not, that's also wonderful! We're *not* here to say some people are better than others; we're here to say some people are different, sometimes in similar ways.

Except Sir Patrick Stewart.
He *is* better than us.

OUR WORDS—DEFINITION OF TERMS

DEFINITIONS ARE BROKEN INTO TWO SECTIONS here, and the third section shows up later:

1. Concepts
2. Roles
3. Identities

Hopefully, setting some definitions for these categories can help us avoid the conflation of words and concepts that tend to create more confusion than clarity. So, when we use these words in this book, here is what we're trying to say...

CONCEPTS

Competence or Skill

A measurement scale for a person's ability to perform well at a task or a set of tasks.

We will use competence (or skill) as not strictly binary—competent or incompetent—but with the allowance for a range. More like a 1–10 scale. The low end of this is "incompetence" or inability to perform a task or set of tasks, and the high end is being highly competent.

Energy

An individual's ability to perform in their roles, independent of competence. Like a stamina meter (a very familiar concept for gamers).

Identity

From Dictionary.com: *Identity is the unique set of characteristics that can be used to identify a person as themselves and no one else. The word can be used in different ways in different contexts.*

We agree with that definition, and for this context we'll add, "An individual's grouping of talents and behavioral tendencies, independent of their role(s)."

Role, Job, or Seat

A role is an empty seat to be filled, or a jacket to be worn. A "job to do," so to speak. Socially defined status or position or expectations that you can put on and take off.

In theater, you could have a role like the "lead." In a business context, Jim Collins' *Good to Great* calls this a "seat." And, also like a jacket, a role can be filled by a person, but it doesn't have to be.

Talent or Trait

Something innate that you're born with—a "natural trait"—like height or hip width or a lot of mental tendencies. Innate (inborn, natural) talents or traits are often referred to as "gifts." In a cross of business and individual context, *Strengths Finder* by Tim Rath speaks of talents as areas within yourself where you have a naturally high capacity for performance.

Examples:

- Perfect Pitch
- Pattern recognition
- Empathy

We believe you have your traits and talents permanently. You can choose to grow them, let them stay dormant, or allow them to wither, but you can't throw them away or take them off.

H2B2

What we nicknamed the overall brand of How to be Second, including this book and the everything else. An "insider" term for the community, if you will. (It's also way more convenient for logo design than the full phrase.)

ROLES

First in Command

A top level job or role in any group of people organized into a hierarchy. Often given the title "CEO" in a business context, but the First in Command role exists almost everywhere, in almost any group.

Some examples of First in Command Roles:

- Pope
- CEO
- President
- Conductor
- Mayor

First in Training (or "First Role, Eventually")

An expectation often embedded into certain roles. In the same way that the role of "Princess" carries the possibility, and sometimes expectation, of an eventual movement into the role of "Queen." The First in Training would be expected to eventually assume the role of First in Command.

Between Batman, Robin, and Alfred, Robin is often seen as filling the "Second in Command Role" or "Right Hand" roles. However, whatever role Robin fills, it comes with some expectation of him being in the First Role, Eventually.

Integrator

A job or role within the EOS system, as introduced by Gino Wickman in the book *Traction*. Typically understood to be a Second in Command type role.

Second In Command

The "right hand" of whoever is First in Command for the organization or group.

COO

Stands for Chief Operating Officer, which is a job or role typically found in larger organizations.

CHAPTER 1

HOW TO BE SECOND

(WHEN NO ONE KNOWS WHAT THAT MEANS)

HOW TO BE SECOND was supposed to be a container in which to put everything that I learned along the path to becoming a fantastic COO.

In Seth Godin's book *The Dip* he talks about becoming "The Best in the World" at something. I've heard advice like that a thousand times before—stuff like "riches in the niches"—and by the time I set out to write this book, I had decided I wanted to be the best COO in the world.

Or the best Chief of Staff. Or Integrator. Or Second in Command. Or General Manager, President, Right Hand...

There actually seemed to be a *lot* of confusion about what exactly my "best" role was supposed to be and what to call it. On top of that, when I started looking into books and other learning material for COOs, there was almost nothing available. At least, nothing compared to resources for CEOs. If I made a pie chart that represented those two data points and fit that chart onto this page, the "COO material" slice wouldn't even be visible. Start looking into specific position titles like President or Chief of Staff or Integrator, and it gets even more scarce.

The COO job descriptions that I did find changed dramatically from org to org, with the most common theme being "expected to become the CEO eventually." Which also didn't seem to fit with what I was looking for. I wasn't trying to become First in Command—I was trying to become better at being Second in Command.

There did seem to be one unifying article about this concept, which was published in the *Harvard Business Review* and fittingly called "Second in Command: The misunderstood role of the chief operating officer." I read this article several times and while It seemed to be a unifying article for people In the COO community, it didn't seem unifying at all to me. It actually described seven completely different purposes for the COO role, some of which felt directly at odds with each other, Including a few that were effectively custom built waiting rooms for eventual CEOs.

The more I dug into my exploration of this role for myself, the more I heard from other people about how confusing it all seemed to be.

Take this story from my friend Mondo Davison, founder of Schoolz:

As a visionary type, I knew I needed a number two, but only out of seeing it being executed elsewhere. The vision in my brain was Zuckerberg and Cheryl. So I was just like, "Yo, I need to find my Cheryl." However, because I've never met a Cheryl, I didn't know her. All these relationships I was building [while] trying to find this person— without an objective understanding of who or what Cheryl Sandberg does or is—was a challenge."

OK, so founder-type people were confused about what this all meant too—but perhaps that was only true in some of the smaller business structures or communities I was part of. After all, the role of COO existed in bigger businesses.

Those organizations were probably very clear on what a COO was and how to be great at it.

Right?

Well, here's a story from Cameron Herold, host of the "Second in Command" podcast, author of the book *Second in Command*, and former COO of 1-800-Got-Junk:

> *So I was at a conference—gosh this was about twelve years ago. Verne Harnish was running an event called the Gazelles, and I was speaking at his event in Atlanta. I was just finishing off my seven years as the COO of 1-800-Got-Junk, and I had just come off the stage when this guy came running up to me and goes "Holy shit, you're Cameron!" I said, "Yeah?" And he goes, "I thought it was a saying! People have been saying 'You need a Cameron' and I thought it was like, 'I need a BHAG,' and 'Core Values.' I didn't know it was a person." And I said, "What are you talking about?" And he said "All these people throughout the EO and YPO world were saying that they needed a Cameron, and they thought it was a thing.*

The first time I heard Cameron tell that story, I admit being a bit discouraged. Even so, *the really huge* companies like IBM, Motorola, Yahoo, Pepsi, Mattel, Xerox had COO positions. So I checked out the book *Riding Shotgun: The Role of the COO*, by Nate Bennett and Miles Stephen. I was a little concerned that "the" book on the topic was published in 2006, since that seemed pretty recent for a position that seemed to have been around for a really, really long time. That was alright, though! These two had interviewed those *top-top* CEOs and COOs and learned what it really meant to be a COO and how to become great at it. I knew they had some answers for me. (You already know where this is headed...)

Here's an excerpt from the end of *Riding Shotgun*:

> *A FINAL WORD—As noted at the outset, our primary goal for this undertaking was to encourage insights that might be used to effectively deploy a COO structure. The most important observation gleaned from the interviews continues to be that the role escapes a single definition, except in the broadest sense as the number two executive.*

...so I was wrong, that actually wasn't helpful at all.

Nobody really knew what this thing was or what to call it? Or what a person *did* once they got there?

Oh, and then I realized that the authors of *Riding Shotgun* were also the authors of that single HBR article about the misunderstood role of the COO. A very small circle of info indeed.

How were people measuring and assessing roles like this, if even the top companies in the world couldn't paint a clear picture of what the role was or what the expectations of it were?

How could someone implement or pursue roles like this, and why would anyone trust that doing so would get them where they wanted to go?

How was I supposed to convince someone that adding me as their "Second in Command" was going to supercharge whatever it was we were doing? How could I possibly train to become this thing or get better at it if I couldn't even acknowledge whether I technically already was or had been in the role? I knew I had some level of competence for what I saw the role doing—and competence was and is very important to me—but I didn't have any avenues to display that competence well.

I wanted to feel valued and communicate that value, but I didn't have language to do so, and I couldn't find that language anywhere.

I remember starting to feel very odd. Like maybe I was a little ignorant fish swimming in a tiny little pond, and I just needed to be exposed to the wider world. After all, it *seemed* like the role was there. People were talking about it the way I was and being given the same titles I was using... except Everythinger, I couldn't find that In a job posting, but it seemed to resonate in conversation! Also, if there was one thing that everyone agreed on throughout all the material that I found, it was just how incredibly valuable that people who performed well in that kind of position were. So, I wasn't dissuaded. I still wanted to be great at it.

During the pandemic, I read *Corona* by Scott Galloway. In it, he says, *"I find the best way to learn about something is to write a book about it."* I took that to mean I should work full-time as an Integrator (Everythinger, etc.), run my little marketing agency on the side, and also start writing a book about this mysterious position and how to be awesome in it.

No problem.

I set out to write a book about how to be awesome at this thing I didn't have a sturdy set of words to describe yet. And since nobody seemed to have a handle on the language around this thing, that issue actually became the first thing to tackle.

I didn't intend to figure it all out on the first shot, but barely scratching the surface is better than whatever it is we have now. I hoped that I could just point out that this kind of role existed, give it a name, and get it on map so we could talk about it. Establish some clarity, you know? And I had joked MANY times over the years about someday writing a book called *How to be Second*. Partly because that's the spot I really loved to be in, and partly because, "Who would want to write that?"

I gave up saying "Integrator" or "President" or "COO." I stopped unironically putting "Generalist" and "Everythinger" in my resume, then bracing myself for the trappings that came with all those titles. I knew what I was *really* trying to say: "The person who seems to happily sit at the right hand of whoever is in charge."

So I encapsulated all of that in the word "Second."

The position that is Second.

The person who is Second.

The work of the Second.

How to be Second.

I decided to learn as much about being "second" as I could, to be as inquisitive and empirical as seemed possible, and to write it all down as I went.

I like to consider myself a voracious learner when my curiosity is piqued—and it definitely was for this—and I tend to find myself doubly inspired to take on projects when there's potential value in cataloging my findings into a system for others to benefit from. Since there was such a dearth of information in general, it seemed like adding my little contribution to the small existing stack could be a pretty big help.

I listened to every Second in Command podcast (over 200 of them now) and hundreds more that had words like "COO" and "Second in Command" and "Integrator" in the titles. (Most of them from fairly short-lived channels.)

I read every book I could find on the topic (which, sadly, was not that consuming).

I got RocketFuel Integrator Academy certified.

I joined Integrator and COO and Chief of Staff forums and whatever mastermind groups I could find.

I got a Second in Command coach.

I sold my marketing agency and found another full-time Second in Command job so I could continue living in the role and gaining hands-on experience.

I started a newsletter so I had an excuse to write about this idea every week.

I started to become known as the Second in Command guy in my network.

I drove my wife and my friends nuts.

At one point along the journey, I got lucky enough to recruit my friend, Dr. David Hartman to help with the project and provide a more rigorous structure to it, and he set about interviewing dozens of people and reading all this material alongside me.

That's when "I" became "we," and has remained so for the rest of the project.

We listened to more podcast episodes. Read books together. Interviewed one another. Took writing weekends together where we spoke endlessly on and around the topic while moving from one Starbucks to another.

We recorded videos and posted them on social media, gathering feedback and comments from people who it resonated with.

We interviewed dozens of other people and recorded it all, including several panel interviews that you'll see snippets of in this writing.

Together, we themed and coded hundreds of thousands of words from the transcriptions of those interviews. And that, along with our discovered quotes, snippets, essays, newsletter writings, personal research, and podcast and book summaries, began to synthesize into something usable.

Something you have in your hands now.

Something still called *How to be Second*.

The name is unchanged, but boy, did we have some surprises along the way.

If you've resonated with anything I've said so far, I think you'll be excited for what we've put together. It's not going to be *the* authoritative text, but I suspect it may be one of the very few that are written just for you—or at least this part of you. I hope you'll enjoy our journey of research and discovery as much as we did and, if this *is* you, that you'll join us and our community in moving forward together.

WHO ARE WE?

David

We come at this topic from different origins—different backgrounds, different training, different temperaments, and different areas of focus. However, we think in very compatible ways. Even when we don't speak exactly the same language, we get the gist of what the other is trying to get across.

I'll go through each of the areas of difference that I spelled out in the beginning of this paragraph, and I think you'll see that our differences make this a more robust book than if either one of us wrote it individually.

Different Backgrounds

If you dial it way back in time, we were raised in homes with parents who had very different careers. Nathan was raised in a family that owned a small local business, and I was raised in a house with two parents who worked mid-level state government jobs. Those occupations of our families of origin definitely show up in our career trajectories.

Nathan's career trajectory has been marked by entrepreneurship and a demand that he figure things out for himself. He constantly sets challenges for himself and learns how to build the path in front of him. What led Nathan to this topic is the fact that, while entrepreneurial, he has never really wanted to be a CEO or First in Command. In fact, when he has done it, he hasn't liked it (even though he was pretty good at it).

He's carved out a niche for himself in operations and, in the last few years, as an Integrator. It was interesting to see him figure out that all of the process analysis and refinement he does just to help himself make sense of things was something that companies desperately needed as well. He's worked in Second in Command roles and as a process consultant for years now, and this is the lens he predominantly views our topic through.

I tend to be more risk averse, but I still don't want to be a cog in a huge wheel. I grow discontent with shoddy processes and incompetent leadership that won't change or can't defend its operational strategies. Nathan and I are both natural researchers, but I tend to be more academic in my research framework where Nathan is more pragmatic. Higher education has been a huge part of my life as both a student and a faculty member.

My background is in sociology, psychology, and counseling, and I blend these disciplines to investigate how people develop and sustain identities. I've worked as a professor and therapist, I have run an innovation lab for developing social programs, and I currently oversee learning and development for a tech firm.

Different Training

I have more of a traditional educational background, as you might have guessed. My undergraduate degrees are in psychology and sociology. I have Master's degrees in sociology and counseling. My Ph.D. is in counseling. I have also studied human-centered design and user-experience design in certificate programs.

Nathan's training has been more autodidactic. He will immerse himself in topics as required to solve a problem in front of him, and this approach has seen him develop a huge repertoire. Nathan founded a successful online marketing agency and largely developed an approach through previous work experience that he improved on. He's great at capturing and narrating processes, and this enables him to manipulate and optimize process frameworks.

Different Temperaments

Nathan and I are both analytical—that's our overlap—but we relate to the world differently. Nathan views the world in more mechanistic and cognitive ways and sees people through the lens of processes. I view the world in a more interpersonal and intrapersonal way and see processes through those lenses.

We both see implications for systems and processes, but the implications we attune to may be different. Nathan is great at thinking through technical logistics, cashflow, and revenue. I am good at thinking about team dynamics, human capacity issues, leadership style, etc. You'll see these differences show up in our writing as you read this book.

Different Areas of Focus

My work has focused on how we establish, refine, and maintain optimal identities. Nathan has sat with issues of the role of Seconds from a technical and logistical frame. When he got to the edge of his thinking about roles, hierarchy, and division of labor between First in Command and Second in Command roles, he started asking more questions about what unique identity aspects of a Second might look like. There's just not enough out there on it. So he contacted me. And then, we wrote this book.

SO, WHAT IS A SECOND?

TO HELP YOU GET A SENSE of the paradigm of a Second, let's look at some accessible examples who flesh out what we're talking about.

Something we hope you'll notice right away is the inclusion of examples that don't carry the COO title. That's because the first thing we found about being Second is that it exists everywhere. This is an important distinction between Seconds and COOs or other similar titles: there seems to be an *inherent* need for this specific set of work to be done, no matter the organizational type. Once you buy into this idea, you start to see Seconds everywhere, including literature, popular culture, and history.

While there are fewer examples historically—cultures have typically been fixated with the record of heroes who take unilateral action and not as much about other characters—they do exist. On every team, this jacket must be worn, and oddly, the person wearing it seems to go largely unrecognized for what they do.

Alfred (Batman's Butler)

This has become a good test for whether someone is grasping the Second concept. If you thought "Robin" when you thought of a Second in Batman's world, you're a little off the scent, and that's common. It was one of our first "aha" moments of distinction as well.

In Alfred, we see someone who runs Batman's affairs and household. Alfred is impeccably loyal to Batman and supportive to a fault. He and Batman have clearly defined lanes of practice and competence that support and depend on each other, while Batman and Robin perform similar or overlapping roles. Remember, Seconds are not a CEO in Training or First, Eventually.

Alfred is an incredible display of what it means to be Second in Command, and he is absolutely *not* sitting around waiting to get called up for his turn in the Batmobile. Rather, he would be the first to make sure that the Batmobile had followed its maintenance schedule, to take feedback from Batman on what performance enhancements the Batmobile needs, or to know how to set the upgrades motion.

Formula One Race Engineers

During the COVID-19 pandemic, many Netflix subscribers became addicted to the *Drive to Survive* docuseries that followed Formula One race drivers through a racing season.

As people who dig Seconds, our attention was immediately drawn not to the driver, but to the person in the driver's ear. They are constantly calling the race, monitoring data, altering racing strategy, and adjudicating what information is vital to relay across the massive race teams behind each Formula One driver.

Race engineers perpetually have the ear of the performer—the person in the limelight—the driver. And the driver is perpetually at the mercy of the real-time data and strategy of the race engineer. Both roles are vital to successful race performances.

Joseph, son of Jacob

Long before language for Seconds existed, Joseph perfectly demonstrated the identity and role in Genesis, the first book of the Bible. Many people know a portion of Joseph's story through the hit musical *Joseph and the Amazing Technicolor Dreamcoat*. If you're unfamiliar, Joseph is an interesting character. He had many older brothers, who in that culture would have had more power and esteem due to their birth position. However, Joseph was his father's favorite, and his jealous brothers sold him into slavery.

The slave traders took Joseph far away from his family home, where Joseph ended up becoming trusted as an advisor. He was running the household affairs of his master when, through a conspiracy, he ended up in jail. Again, while in jail, he became trusted as an overseer and began running the jail for his new master. Ultimately, he came to be known and trusted by the ruler of Egypt, a massive empire at the time.

The Pharaoh (ruler) of Egypt, entrusted Joseph as administrative ruler, and some texts literally read that Joseph was Pharaoh's "second in command." Joseph oversaw administrative programs and planning (there is evidence of his running a food distribution program during a famine) and wielded significant power. But it was clear he was a complement to Pharaoh's reign, not a rival or threat.

Cheryl Sandberg—COO, Facebook

Much has been written about Cheryl Sandberg, and it would be hard not to recognize the name or her contribution to the powerhouse that was Facebook, before it became Meta. If you say "Second in Command" or "COO," it's easy to point to Cheryl Sandberg and see what is possible when you pair the roles of CEO and COO together effectively.

From 2008 to 2022, she managed the company's business operations, among other things, from her role as COO. Arguably, Cheryl could have and did build an empire all on her own, but in our time spent reading about Cheryl, we noticed a repeated keystone that everyone has touched on: how critical being in lock-step with Zuckerberg (the First in Command) really was.

The Right Hand Man (or Foil) Trope

Our favorite place for the breakdown on this version of Seconds is the YouTube channel Overly Sarcastic Productions, in which they have a long-running series of videos called "Trope Talk." The Lancer and Right Hand Man videos are awesome.

It would be a shame to chop their wonderful videos into tiny, bite-sized explanations here, so now that I've mentioned them as a premier source, I'll simply offer this definition quoted from TVTropes.com:

> *The right-hand man of The Leader, or second in command. Usually The Lancer and a Foil. The one who takes over the "ship" when The Captain wants to be off doing non-Captainy things.*
>
> *Often called simply Number Two (or, confusingly, Number One), although terms like "first officer," "first mate," or "executive officer" (often shortened to "XO")*

frequently appear in military fiction especially involving the chain of command in a Command Roster. Compare The Lancer in the Five-Man Band, who is usually not too happy about that. Although sometimes the Number Two is also The Lancer to provide a contrast between authority figures. In-universe this is also a good idea: If The Leader is Hot-Blooded then he needs The Stoic to balance him, and vice versa.

If the creators did the research, the XO is much more likely to interact with the crew. On a ship, "Number One" is responsible for the crew: training, ordinary discipline (that is motivating the NCOs to motivate the others) setting watches for the officers etc. The captain's job is to decide what the ship should do, Number Two makes sure the ship and crew can do it.

If the Number Two is also the final obstacle before reaching the Big Bad, then they're The Dragon. Sometimes gets "promoted" to Commander Contrarian. The dimwit version is Number Two for Brains. If they double as the voice of reason, they're The Consigliere.

The Consigliere

If you've seen the Godfather movies, you'll remember Tom Hagen, consigliere to Vito Corleone. Played by Robert Duvall, Tom Hagen is a cunning negotiator and trusted confidante to the mob boss—and an excellent showcase of the loyalty of a Second.

Tom, trusted for his discretion and strategic wit, enables the Corleone family to build their empire and recognize their strategic vision. As Tom gets moved to the periphery of dealings, you also see what happens to a Second when they lose the trust of their First in Command. It's not pretty.

Perhaps surprisingly, the Consigliere is a real position in mafia families and effectively performs a role in step with what's displayed in *The Godfather*. The word literally means "counselor" or "adviser" in Italian. Supposedly the term is still a title for city council positions.

Virginia (Pepper) Potts, *Iron Man*

In the Marvel Cinematic Universe, we primarily see Pepper Potts in her role as personal assistant to Tony Stark, and what she's actually capable of operationally is sort of left to assumption. But she must have nearly untouchable levels of "get stuff done," as she's trusted implicitly as the Right Hand of the entire Stark organization.

Eventually, Tony promotes her to CEO over Stark Industries so he can live in his roles as the genius Iron Man Avenger (and because he felt like he was going to die soon after). And then she totally *does* run Stark Industries by herself, effectively taking over as an insanely capable business operations leader where Tony had been a more traditional a visionary-genius-spotlight type who's reliant on capable operations people...like Pepper.

Mr. Carson, *Downton Abbey*

In this beloved period piece, Mr. Carson heads the downstairs staff. He also enjoys the trust *and* the ear of Lord Grantham, the head of the manor. We see that Carson (as the Grantham family refers to him) enjoys his privileged role, being privy to considerably more family business than the rest of the staff. And he repays that access with discretion and unshakable loyalty.

Seconds can be incredible champions and establishers of company culture, and Carson represents this well. The collective is the most important thing to Carson—Downton is a living, breathing amalgam that provides ultimate meaning to him. Downton is both a physical reality and an ideal that Carson embodies and defends.

Honorable Mentions

- Roy Disney to Walt Disney
- John Watson to Sherlock Holmes
- Sid McGee to Shea McGee
- Ben Wyatt to Chris Traeger
- Pieter Mulier to Raf Simons
- Samwise Gamgee to Frodo Baggins
- Shawn Pilot to Mark Towle
- Spock to Kirk
- Cameron Herold to Brian Scudamore
- Donna Paulsen to Harvey Specter
- Merlin to King Arthur

CHAPTER 3

IT'S A PERSON!

In the biological world, some species are categorized as generalists, who cover a large territory and face more competition, but are flexible in meeting their [own] needs. Others are specialists, who occupy a smaller territory and face less competition but are more rigid in their requirements. Both are vulnerable in their own ways. It is not always better to be one or the other, but knowing which you are can help you strategize your continued survival.

—Peter Unger, The Great Mental Models, Vol. 2

HAVE YOU EVER TAKEN A DRINK of something you thought was one thing, and then it was *not* that thing?

Have you ever put a puzzle together where you didn't know what the picture was until you got it all snapped together and then stepped back to look at it?

While we were writing this book, both of those things happened to us.

As we put together all the puzzle pieces we gathered from our research, we stepped back and stared at the creation in front of us...

...and then we both spat out the orange-juice-we-thought-was-coffee and shouted, "HOLY ****! That's a PERSON?!?"

STORYTIME!

Nathan

You know those masters of their craft who started when they were just a little kid? And sometimes you think, *Well, if I had started my thing when I was that young, I'd be that great too!* Even though I started working in the family business when I was very young—which allowed a lot of hours working right away—I've been frustrated by thoughts like that a lot in my life.

From ten years old to my early twenties, no matter how hard I tried to focus on one thing, I got pulled into all the connecting stuff, through capacity or curiosity or necessity. It drove my dad crazy, and it felt like there was no way I could ever become a master. My curiosity had squandered all my time! What's that quote from Bruce Lee about not fearing the person who had done 10,000 kicks one time but instead fearing the person who had done one kick 10,000 times? It felt like I was doing 10,000 different kicks. I worked different jobs and filled different roles at those jobs and played in bands and volunteered for multiple organizations and joined online gaming guilds and started and ran my own micro-companies, all without ever "finding my thing."

Eventually, I noticed that I was falling into the same spot again and again and again—and I *really* liked that spot! At some point, I knew I had found the thing I could master and enjoy, and I decided that what I really wanted was to be the best Second in Command in the world. (And yes, I did realize how odd it is to say I wanted to be the number one Second in Command. *You and I* understand those are different things, especially now—but it is funny to say. Even to me.) Except I had no idea how to SAY that. And neither did anyone around me.

During those agonizing years, I actually found a full-time job as a "Second in Command", even though my bosses literally couldn't figure out what title to give me. The owners I worked for just said, "We've never had a Nathan before." I asked to be Project Manager and to get promoted to General Manager if things worked out. Back in my twenties, I had read *The E-myth Revisited*, which said certain people existed naturally as "Managers." That language didn't quite fit, but it was something to work from. To learn more, I tried reading about all sorts of generalist positions and manager positions, leading to my maddeningly disappointing discovery of the title "General Manager." Salaries for the role topped out at about $45k a year, already a low wage compared to what I was making as just a generalist consultant. And, as always, the description just... didn't ... fit, you know?

I didn't want to be a General Manager, but it felt like the most "correct" thing I could come up with, and the most honest to what I did.

The company grew fairly quickly, and it was *fun*. I loved my bosses, my team, and my work. One of the owners and I truly found that First and Second in Command fit. People would ask me how things were at work and I'd say, "It's insane, and I love it."

A few years in, some things changed, and the First in command left the company. I didn't know at the time why that felt like a full-on gut punch. After almost a year of straight awfulness, I found the book *Traction*, and the word Integrator. I actually cried the first time I read it, *because it felt like I found myself,* as a person. I've told this story a bunch of times, and I like to say, "When I was twelve, I found Jesus, and in my twenties I found Gino. And both of them changed my life."

Remembering how emotional I felt while reading that book is funny to me now. There's almost nothing to describe *the person* in Traction. It just describes the role and job duties of the Integrator. But the description was *exactly* the work I had done in the positions I had ended up in my whole life. Having a word to encapsulate that thing I kept doing—and confirmation that it had a high value at much higher levels of businesses and organizations—was incredibly empowering. It opened the floodgates to my education. I started reading about roles like Chief Operations Officer and Chief of Staff and basically anything I could get my hands on.

As usual for me, I found a mentor in this area as quickly as possible. I will be forever grateful to him. *(Brian, I am incredibly thankful for your generous heart and spending time with me and teaching me. I keep the last of the books with your sticker in it on my shelf like a signed copy of some treasured novel. Your mentorship and investment were as much or more impactful to me as reading the book in the first place.)*

Brian challenged me right away with the question, "Do you want to be an Implementer or an Integrator?" I knew that I could do either, but I also knew that I wanted to *commit* to the Integrator path. For a while I did, sticking to the

EOS stomping grounds and finding a job with the title Integrator in a company that ran on the EOS system, while and consulting as a "Fractional Integrator." It mostly worked, and it definitely scratched the second in command itch!

But.

When you create a role and say it's super valuable, people start molding themselves to fit into that role. And people are really flexible! So while I was shaping myself to be the best possible version of this thing someone else had created, I heard people start saying things like, "Well, I'm more Integrator than Visionary," immediately followed by, "I'm a Visionary, but I can do both." Traction was published In 2007 and was still only cult popular, and people were already tearing at these definitions to fit their own uses.

It wasn't long before in-groups and out-groups started to form. Statements like, "I'm not just qualified, I'm *the person*" picked up as people began vying (usually kindly) for status and respect as the "true" thing, rather than just someone who could do project management type work or was sort of organized.

I watched people using this word, Integrator, to *identify* themselves. Not just a role they lived in for a moment in time, but as a way to explain their being—who they were as a person, at their core.

And, while watching all of that unfold (with some frustration and concern) I still wanted to be awesome at this thing. Honestly, the idea of having to leave behind one of the few concepts that seemed like it was starting to help others understand and value who I was, only to start all over on my own, was somewhere between terrifying and exhausting. You probably know what I mean. But now that there was a word for me to define a role within a defined system, people were *still* struggling with it. It was time to get out or triple down—and I chose to triple down.

Several of the people David and I interviewed shared similarly dramatic stories. Some were in those types of roles already, and some were not. It didn't make much sense at the time, but now it seems obvious.

As I've mentioned, *How to be Second* was supposed to be a container to store everything that I learned while reading and talking to people in order to define the role and how to be great at it. And as David and I talked, interviewed, listened to the community—as we read what was available and themed and coded hundreds of thousands of words from our own interviews, one thing became impossible to ignore:

This wasn't just a role. There was a person here. An identity.

Authors like Gino Wickman, W. Edwards Deming, Michael Gerber, Jim Collins, Verne Harnish, and Simon Sinek (among many others) had outlined the need for this particular role to be filled, sometimes going as far as saying there were these sort-of-rare people in the world who really *fit* into the role... and leaving it at that.

Can you imagine if a personality test gave you sixteen results, but the assessment only described the details for fifteen of the types? And the sixteenth one was just like "We see you, but we don't know what words to give you to describe yourself or communicate who you are to other people. Best of luck!"

Bewilderment is probably a good word to use here.

All throughout our research, we found this growing issue of trying to place people who seemed like the right fit for these Second in Command roles, but then they... weren't? And how could a CEO really tell, anyway? We watched a lot of people failing in the role. Their CEOs were frustrated and felt like they were "getting it wrong." We heard things like, "They're in the seat, but they don't really 'get it,' y'know?"

We watched some thought leaders in the space point to maturity curves, saying people can grow into the role and that failing to "get it" is exclusively an issue of experience. But that just doesn't hold up with our understanding of human talent and capacity.

We also watched some recruiting firms claim to have cracked the code on "actually knowing who these people are," via interviewing processes and batteries of assessments and other tools. But if it were just a *role* we needed to define, none of that would make any sense. You don't need a personality test for a role; you need a resume.

To be fair, a great same-page relationship between the CEO and COO *is* super important for the roles, but even then we're talking about person-to-person fit. We're outside the bounds of being qualified for a role based on experience and *all the way* into being qualified for a role based on *who you are*.

What REALLY broke the whole thing was that we had conversations with a bunch of people who weren't in the business world at all, had never heard the word Integrator, and barely knew (or didn't know) what a "COO" was or did... *and those people fit perfectly into the shape we had drawn for seconds.* As if they were just born that way. *And* some people were saying I was born this way" anyway.

Eventually, we admitted that the book couldn't be about the role. It's the identity that matters to us, because there *is* one, and someone needs to talk about it.

ADDITIONAL TERMS: IDENTITIES

Because we're bringing in specific words for this idea of "Second" as a type of person who is naturally suited to certain kinds of work and has natural tendencies to do that work—we need to provide some identifiers. Clues for people who (we feel) don't really fit into that Second-type role, but bump up against it all the time. AKA everyone else. We're breaking it down like this...

Second

A group of people who seem to have a particular identity—that is, a grouping of talents and behavioral tendencies—independent of their roles, outlined in as much detail as possible within *How to be Second* (the book you're reading right now).

Artisan

A person who desires to achieve very high levels of competence in a job, and has both the desire and energy to become a ten out of ten.

Artisans are typically very well-educated, practiced, and experienced in their chosen job, as well as talented. In sales, we call these "Rainmakers."

A few examples of artisans:

- Lionel Messi (footballer/soccer player)
- Grace Hopper (computer scientist)
- Jiro Ono (sushi chef)
- Victor Wooten (musician/bass guitarist)

Contributor

Everyone else.

Typically, the definition of Contributor is "a person or thing that contributes something," and in that sense, Seconds are *also* Contributors.

Why use this word then?

Specifically *because* Contributor normally encapsulates everyone, including Seconds. We're all Contributors, and in this book we deal with subgroups. So we'll acknowledge the broader group, then give sub-groups specific, extra words.

WHO WE ARE

We're saying that we discovered this concept was a person and not a role, but what does it sound like to be that person outside of Nathan's story?

When we did all those interviews, lots of people told us their own stories!

We've included a few of them below to show that it's not just Nathan who is this thing, it is who WE are. Who *Seconds* are.

Please enjoy these interview excerpts from a few fellow Seconds.

The following are excerpts from a panel interview with the Catalyst Fractional Integrator team, a group of women who serve as part time Integrators for companies running on the EOS system. Interview conducted by Nathan Young.

Nathan: Do we all agree that you might be a natural Integrator type without ever having held the role, and in fact that you could be a natural Integrator type without being in *any* business structure?

Catalyst Team: Yeah. Yes. Mmhmm.

Nathan: Cool. I want to ask this question next then:

I've heard all of these stories, and I also have this story of reading a book and finding that who I was had a word. That was so significant, so life changing, because someone had codified who I already was into a word that other people could understand and find value in. It didn't mean it changed who I was, but it allowed me to finally anchor my identity to a word.

But if that's true, then you must have been doing this before that, right? If you had that moment of clarity when you're like, "Yes, this is the thing!" then you existed that way before you got there. The colors were the colors before you could see, right?

When did you first realize that you might be someone who is naturally suited to a Second or Second in Command type role? And how did it happen?

Lisa McCurdy: For me, it was super organic. I just found, any time I would start with an organization, I always rose up in the ranks very quickly, and I always rose to that second role, supporting. It doesn't matter the industry, because I worked in multiple industries. But that was just kind of the natural progression of me rising through the ranks or me getting hired into that role. I would always joke and say like, "I'm the get shit done person." Like, if you have something that needs to happen, if there is a plan that needs to get executed, they just give it to me and it was done.

So that was the language I used before EOS: I get it done. When people would ask me what I do, I was like, "I get it done." I just do it; I make it happen. And then when EOS came, I was already in a Second in Command role, and my Visionary handed me the book and was like, "Let's do this." And I was like, "I don't even know what that means, but okay." In my standard, get-it-done mentality, we self-implemented and then brought Jamie in to help us take it the rest of the way. It was just really organic. It just always happened. It was just who I innately was.

Paulina Walters: I feel like mine was not as organic as I wish it was. Early in my career, I started consulting, and when I was consulting, I was always the Right Hand person to the owner of the consulting company. But my title was not Integrator or, you know, right hand, right? It was just "associate consultant."

It was weird that I always got hired for a role, but within six months I always got promoted to this other role where it was like, *I'm more working on the business?* I was hired to just do a specific role in the business, but I guess through my unique ability I was always asking, "Well, how are we doing in terms of goals?" and "How's this department doing?" I never stood in my silo where I was supposed to. I was always like, "How are we doing overall as an organization?"

So throughout my career I was always unofficially working with owners, Visionaries, really helping them build and scale their companies. Like most of us on this call, I was handed the book *Traction* when I landed a Director of Operations role here in Dallas, and the visionary was like, "I heard about this cool new system—can you start on it tomorrow and get it done by the end of the week?" And I was like, "Sure, how hard can it be?"

So officially that's when I knew. I don't know if [I knew] it was an identity, because all I've ever known is how to operate the way that I do. But when I read *Integrator*, it was more like, "I'm not alone." It was an inclusive thing. When I work in an organization, there are departments of people and they know where they fit in. For me, I was just everywhere, you know? ...So I think when I read *Traction*, it was like, "Wow, there's other people like me...There's actually a role." So that was kind of my upbringing into the Integrator seat.

Nicole Mennicke: I started with a digital marketing agency back in 2008, and in 2012, I became a director of a department. So there were two departments—PPC and SEO—and I was leading the paid media department.

As a company, we had the same goals and vision, but over six years the two [departments] were run so differently. So my department, years before I even read the book *Traction*, we had process and training. We had data and square card metrics and measurables. We had people and role clarity. We had goal setting. It's like I ran a little mini-empire, even though it was the same goal. And my counterpart on the other side just didn't have all those things in place.

I think like Paulina, it's like I naturally gravitated towards, "Okay, well then what can we put in place?" And everyone knew what we were doing and had our own celebrations. And I think when we read *Traction*, we looked at the two departments. And my department was 70 percent of revenue, the other department was 30 percent of revenue. I think it was like, *wow*, ...I was just kind of running this department on EOS without knowing about EOS because I was just naturally inclined to it.

Kristyn Drennen: I would say, very early on in my career, really in any position I've ever held, I've always naturally gravitated towards being in those types of Second in Command, leadership-type positions.

I'm trying to think—I think it's not since I was maybe in college that I even held a position as an employee in a non-leadership position. Every job, listening to you explain it, every position I've ever held has been a leadership position. And if I started in a company in a non-leadership position, I've elevated very, very quickly.

I think the other thing there is, you talk about this concept of a natural Integrator regardless of system, and I think that's very consistent with when you see natural leaders that pop up inside of organizations regardless of title. Their voice carries that weight, where people listen to them.

If they champion something, others very easily follow. And I think people that have that natural Integrator skillset or that Second in Command skillset, they are just so obvious.

I think it's why many of us are so successful in this fractional seat as well, because we're the people who, when we go into a company, everyone looks at us and goes, "I want her to do something great for my company," right? And they don't even necessarily know where to put you, but they know that you have that special sauce and that you're gonna bring something wonderful and help elevate the organization.

Nathan: So far, we're five for five on, "I accidentally would work my way up to the thing every single place I went." Jamie, you're the only one who hasn't answered yet.

Jamie Munoz: I'd probably say ditto to a lot of everything that's already been shared. I think for all of us, like I was saying with Lisa earlier, it's coming it to "Why, though?" Why were you, Kristyn, put into leadership right away? Why, Nicole, were you trusted to be put in that seat right away?

We all share that same story, that we did something or they saw something in us, which—I'm assuming this is where we're headed with this, Nathan—is like, what are the traits or like what are the things at the root that give business owners or visionaries or whoever the confidence to know that they can trust us. What do we do?

The following are excerpts from a panel interview with Mondo Davison, founder of Schoolz; Beth Carr, founder of Fortified Branding; Skyler Werde, then Vice President of Operations at Lola Red; and Jeff Kubiatowicz, Fractional Integrator and previously founder of Red Galoshes. Interview conducted by Nathan Young and David Hartman.

Jeff Kubiatowicz, on finding himself after living in a role that didn't fit.

Jeff Kubiatowicz: Two pieces here.

One: The consequences of my being "misdiagnosed" [as *not* a Second] are very, very, very real. At the end of my mis-diagnosis, I was officially clinically depressed, to the point where people were concerned about my wellbeing. I joke around a lot, but it was pretty freaking serious, what was going on in my life. So I think, sure, you can write a how-to business book, but there is some very serious emotional content under that, of being misidentified. Because really what happens is I'm bringing my best gifts to the table—and I'm being told where I can stick it. And if I hear that enough times, my self-esteem goes absolutely in the toilet. And you do that long enough, you're depressed, and it's very bad. So that's how I walked into this thing.

Two: When I started getting into EOS, I was like, I smell something here. This smells like me. And when it hit was when I was in one of these Zoom things with a bunch of people who were like me, and I spotted this kid who seemed like he really had his stuff together. And I gave him a call and we connected. So the recovery from my depression was built on, yes, a book, but more a community, and more on my relationships with other people who didn't think I was a complete jerk.

David Hartman: Yeah, that's good. I mean, I have a touch-point there too. One of the reasons I'm working on this book project with Nathan is that I hate being in academia because most of the time I'm by myself. If I'm not teaching class, I am alone, and the administration is like, "Do research," which is what a lot of folks do that work full time as Profs. And it's depressing. I mean that speaking as a therapist, as someone who has clinical depression in their family—I run really low when I don't get to collaborate. And when I'm not doing what I'm supposed to do. So I can do the academic thing well, but yeah, I get that. Absolutely.

The following is an excerpt from an interview with Kristie Clayton, then Integrator of BCR Wealth Strategies and founder of Female Integrator Mastermind (FIM). Interview conducted by Nathan Young.

Nathan: When did you first realize you might be—I'm gonna call it a Second in Command. When was the first time that you were like, "I think I might be a Second in Command; I think that might be the role for me"?

Kristie: Yeah. It's interesting. You know, looking back at my career, it's more than obvious that I've sat in the Second in Command role many times.

I think the big difference, previous to being at BCR, is we didn't have an operating system. We didn't have rules of engagement—of, "Hey, this is your lane, this is my lane, here's how we work together, here's how we make things happen." It's always been in me, but previously it was always a question of, "What am I doing?" Like, why is this not working? Why is it a struggle? Why am I constantly like feeling like my toes are just being stepped on, that I'm bumbling through this, but it should be so easy? There really should be something that makes this easy.

When I got the role at BCR... First of all, I did not know I was being hired for the Integrator. I was being hired for an Operations Manager. They were doing all the interviews, and the questions they were asking me, the assessments that I was taking—all of it was for an Integrator.

I accepted the role, and then they sent me *Traction* and *Rocket Fuel*. I just remember sitting on my couch on a Saturday, and my Visionary had sent it to me. He said, "Hey, read this before you start, because I want you to know our operating system and how we work." And I remember sitting there reading *Traction*, reading *Rocket Fuel*, tears just flowing down my face because I finally had an identity.

You know, my previous Visionaries—and it's clear I've always worked for Visionaries or First in Commands, as you wanna call 'em—they always called me a weirdo. *Why do you care about that? What are you trying? I don't understand you.* Yep. It's because we didn't have a system. We didn't know how to work cohesively together. Instead, we were constantly fighting each other.

So, when I was reading *Traction* and reading through *Rocket Fuel* it was just an aha moment for me of, "Oh my gosh, I'm not a weirdo." I'm not some strange person. I have an identity. It's this Integrator, and now I have the tools and the resources to become the best Integrator that I can be.

Here's Jeff Kubiatowicz again, along with Nathan, riffing on natural traits of Seconds.

Jeff Kubiatowicz: So, I've known this guy for going on ten years here, and we've had our spins. We have a very direct relationship. In my last job that I bailed, though, I had to be super delicate with the boss, because there was some ego there, and fundraising was not her sweet spot. So I had to flex, and I think it depends.

There's a certain amount of chameleon in me that allows me to flex to who I'm working with. The principle of meet them where they're at—when I can do that, I'm better. I'm not always great at it, but it works better when I do that. So my current guy, he'll take it, but not everybody does.

Nathan Young: I saw myself and Skyler—you and I were both nodding our heads, and Beth and Mondo were both like, "Hmm, interesting."

Skyler on assessments and his own fit.

Skyler Werde: I will have to throw this out—my wife would kill me if I didn't—but the Kolbe assessment is actually designed to do this instinctually. "Where are you? And why are you driven in that way?" (She's a certified Kolbe consultant.) But it's more than just the test; it's interpreting it in a way that matches with the intent of the job.

My Kolbe actually is not directly in line with what an Integrator is supposed to have. So, before I took my current role, we did the assessment for my Visionary to say, "Okay, where are we gonna struggle? Where is that gonna overlap?" And it made it so much easier going in, because then I brought in a partner to cover up my issues. I have a much stronger accounting team because I'm not a fact finder. I'm not gonna be—I mean, I could bring a system and make it work beautifully, but I need to have that support as well.

CHAPTER 4

THE BASE IDENTITY OF A SECOND

IF SECONDS ARE PEOPLE WHO SHARE IDENTITY, traits, and tendencies, then what are the basic contours of someone who would identify as a Second? While it's hard to be exhaustive, we feel confident in at least drawing some crude maps to see if you can find yourself in this general categorization or not.

Perhaps most importantly, here is what we did not find:

- Being Second is not more common in men or women
- Being Second is not more common in introverts or extroverts
- Being Second is not a specific personality assessment type
- Being Second is not related to a particular background
- Seconds are not exclusively found in business environments

What we did find again and again:

- Seconds are team-focused
- Seconds are collaborative
- Seconds are more generalist in skillset
- Seconds have a high willingness to serve
- Seconds have no issue with hierarchy—they even appreciate it and seek it out
- Seconds have similar things that activate their creativity and interest

- Seconds put a high emphasis on moving forward with a plan
- Seconds see causes and implications
- Seconds tend to avoid the spotlight unless needed

To get a bit more granular, we did not find the identity or talents of Seconds to be more commonly prevalent in men or women, but in America we have seen more men in Second in Command or COO roles. And again, we're breaking those concepts apart—Identity does not equal Role.

There's been some chatter about certain results from popular personality tests being high indicators of a good fit for roles like COO. Some examples are "INTJ" or "INTP" from Myers Briggs, "Connectedness" or "Relational" from Strengths Finder, "High C" from DiSC, or low "quick start" from Kolbe. The stereotypical concept of an introvert and the traits we've found for Seconds do have a lot of overlap, but they're not the same. We've seen a lot of extrovert tendencies overlap with the traits of Seconds as well.

Agree or disagree, we're simply saying we've seen many instances where someone is the picture of a Second as far as we can tell, who says of themselves, "That's absolutely me, I'm a Second," while also having results like ENTP and high quick-start.

We're really going to push into those common traits here, even going as far as to call them "Cornerstone" traits. Basically, the traits that we feel almost all people who would identify as a Second would share. And we really are saying that if you're a Second, you probably have *all* of these traits, or really close. The identity is the combination of these things, not just relating to a couple of them.

CORNERSTONE TRAITS

Activation

In terms of what activates the creativity, ingenuity, and interest of a Second: it starts in human relationship. Seconds are activated by the spark of vision from another person (or possibly group of people). This is especially true in terms of both competence and confidence.

Seconds are naturally competent and are often called out for it early in life by being great contributors to group projects at school. They may find themselves in charge of teams in early career jobs. However, if you want to see a Second at their most competent *and* confident, it will be when they are partnering with someone that they respect and who respects them.

Competence

When it comes to performance, accurate representation of competence is a big deal. Seconds often have a huge need to prepare and learn (and create systems/processes—see "Moving Forward with a Plan" below) to make them feel as if they can perform at a high level of competence in their role. In fact, they believe that is what is expected/required to be part of a team.

Others may look at Seconds and perceive high competence already, but Seconds have a *very* high bar for their subjective sense of the competence scale. You'll often find that Seconds will spend a lot of time learning context and underlying information.

Seconds are naturally curious, but this curiosity is often sparked by the drive for competence. Others can become impatient at a Second's "slow start" or perceived "failure to get onboard" with the idea, but this preparation typically pays off in the end.

Moving Forward with a Plan

Seconds have a lot of questions about the plan. This can be perceived as a slow start by some, but in actuality the Second is starting right away—with clarification, so they can take action. Their questions do connect to their outsized need to feel competent, but primarily serve to set up the Second's favorite identity byproduct: systems and processes.

A Second doesn't like to move forward without a plan—in fact, there is no way forward without one. Such is the need they feel for understanding that Seconds will likely configure roles, workflows, SOPs, process maps, etc. for a whole enterprise or team, on their own if necessary. While impatient colleagues may wish that Seconds moved more quickly, these tendencies towards system and process creation usually benefit those around them.

Seeing Causes and Implications

Whether it's a team scratching their heads at why a company is losing profits or a friend struggling to see why they can't find a job, Seconds dig for (and typically find) underlying causes. When a Second hears a superior lay out a new vision or program or a friend describe their issue, the Second will have lots of questions. In part, because they are trying to formulate a plan. But prior to that, it's because Seconds process information in terms of implications. And not just the immediate, knee jerk implications—Seconds see processual load shifts, bottlenecks, and the many downstream effects of a potential change.

Seeing What's There and What's Missing (Not Either/Or)

Flowing from their need to move forward with a plan, Seconds also have a knack for taking process and system inventories. If they sit with a problem long enough, a Second will be able to identify the missing people and portions of processes surrounding the problem. A Second's brain tends to run on internal or external diagrams and visualizations of processes—they may need to externalize a system or process to "think over it" and even manipulate parts of it to address gaps.

Existing Outside of the Spotlight

Seconds are not typically eager to be in the spotlight. There's energy to be had for a Second for a successful performance, but it's typically in the details coming off perfectly and the team being successful overall, rather than the notoriety of being a performer. Oftentimes, if you find Seconds in First in Command roles, you'll discover that there was an outsized need for something to exist, rather than an "opportunity" or chance to be a star.

Followership

Seconds excel at being followers, especially first followers. This needs some nuance. Maybe a whole chapter of nuance. Maybe a *couple* chapters. (This is more foreshadowing, if that wasn't clear. More chapters on followership are coming up soon.)

CHAPTER 5

THERE'S TWO!!!

REMEMBER A FEW CHAPTERS AGO, when we talked about stepping back from what we had pieced together, spitting out the orange-juice-we-thought-was-coffee, and realizing "it" was a person all along?

Can you even imagine what it was like to do that *twice*? (It's a mess)

For the first six months of interviews, stories, discussions, writing, and transcribing, we were anchored to the original target—how to become amazing at this Second in Command thing. It seemed incredible (and obvious in hindsight, of course) to realize that *thing* was an identity. A type of person existed and was doing the work every day as a sort of unsung hero.

At first, when we talked about being Second as an identity, people around us cheered. We had really hit on something we could gather around! That *is* us!

However, the more we discussed it, those same people who at first were so excited to hear this word "Second" and really identify with it seemed to begin displacing themselves to either side of an aisle. It was startling, actually, like feeling confident of your grip on a handful of sand, only to realize it's leaking out all over the place.

For a little while, we had no idea what was going on. We felt like we had missed something critical, which was daunting, since we were pretty deep into uncharted territory already.

The conversations didn't stop, though—we pressed on, listening more, talking more, watching more videos, sending and reading more emails, having more conversations. At some point (*after* the first draft of this book), we built out a little graphic that we call "When Do You See," and things suddenly clicked into place.

There are two people here.

Two people?

...isn't that slicing a bit thin? Were we really just admitting some ignorance?

Well, as we like to say, *stuff can be two things*.

If we admit that identity is really important, and so important that we should anchor to it, then the *nuance* of that identity also matters.

We huddled up, re-organized, told each other we were stupid and/or being egotistical, dismissed it... and kept having conversations. As we did, we used this thinner language. Separating out the two different kinds of people who seemed to share a core, but with very unique edges separating them.

That got a reaction.

The first set of reactions we noticed were within other people—instead of people hearing us talk about Seconds and distancing themselves, we were able to get even more specific about their likely traits and behaviors, including their struggles. Weirdly, they felt almost exposed. Some got upset. Like, *whoa*, upset.

Without intending to, we were bumping against some deep fears. Some of these people were living in roles they didn't quite fit in, and here come these two guys insinuating that maybe it wasn't just training and maturity they were struggling with, but their own natural tendency.

At the same time, we talked with people who were straight up relieved. It's like their whole world seemed to click into place. From "Oh, *that's* why I've hit my head on these types of things," to *"that's* why I surround myself with these kinds of people" and *"that's* why I'm so much better at this than my friends who seem the same."

And then we felt the reaction for ourselves.

David

When Nathan approached me about doing this book with him, my orientation to the material was very much as an outsider. It sometimes feels like Nathan and I are more different than similar in how we think and see the world, but there's a weird overlap that makes us able to "click" in our thinking. Plus, it's fun to work with friends on projects. I figured that given our differences, our research would be slanted towards helping figure out people who were predominantly like Nathan. Basically, I thought, "This will be nice to use my research background to help Nathan figure himself out."

So noble of me. So selfless.

Fast forward to the thick of synthesizing, coding, and poring over our interview transcripts. Any illusions of altruism on my part gave way to interest, then became dangerously close to navel gazing. We basically began to see an archeology of the common space that Nathan and I share, and the two distinct directions people gravitate from that common foundation. Nathan went one direction. I went the other.

I identified deeply with what we saw as the core qualities of "Secondness." I see in processes and implications. I despise poor processes and make sense of the world by creating systems. I prefer following, but I have high standards for those whom I choose to follow. The list went on. Whatever this general "Secondness" was... it was me.

But I didn't like spending as much time looking at combinations of systems and processes across the complexity of an entire organization. I could go there, but I didn't want to live there. And unlike Nathan, I did not want to lead at the highest levels of an organization. I wanted to work with people and form processes. Nathan prefers to work with processes, and working with people is a byproduct. I want to build and coach a team. Nathan wants to orchestrate hirings and firings and move people into the right seats across an organization so that the whole complex of systems and processes becomes efficient and smart.

The more we saw our differences springing out of a common foundation, we also began to see the people that we interviewed drifting in one of our general directions.

We found these constellations of features pointing to more than just roles we could play well in an organization. They are not skills, per se, but abilities, sensibilities, and innate preferences. The closest construct we could find to encapsulate them was that of identities. They are who we are, regardless of the role we step into. They explain what we gravitate toward and away from. They explain our frustrations and enjoyment, and they predict the settings where we flourish and struggle.

They are, at a fundamental level, a vital way of explaining who we are.

It has become incredibly, personally useful to both of us. And I did not expect that.

I'm a Second and so is Nathan—but as we've landed on calling them, I am a 2, and Nathan is a 2iC.

ADDITIONAL, ADDITIONAL TERMS: IDENTITIES

Yeah, we know that doing this again is a bit cheeky, but that's just us sometimes. We're also showcasing a bit how hard it is to name things with unique names that are also descriptive, especially when you have to backtrack on your own conventions as you make new discoveries.

In this (last, we promise) set of additional terms and nuance, we're breaking apart the term Second into its constituent parts. Effectively, we're staking our claim that Second is an umbrella term for two unique identities, which share a significant portion of their traits while having enough differences to be called different things.

Kind of how a baseball and a soccer ball and a basketball are all round balls used for a sport, but each of them is unique in their own right.

Seconds

An umbrella term for a group of people who seem to have a particular identity—that is, a grouping of talents and behavioral tendencies, independent of their roles. Includes both of the unique identities we've found so far, which share the cornerstone traits outlined in chapter 4 of *How to be Second*.

We'll try to stick to using the term Second to include both types of seconds from now on when we use it, though we'll continue attempting to drop in structural reminders by saying things like "both types of Seconds" etc.

2s

One of the unique types of Seconds. The majority of the Seconds population are represented by 2s. The ways that 2s are unique are outlined in detail in chapters 7 and 9 of *How to be Second*.

2iCs

One of the unique types of Seconds. A small portion of the total population of Seconds are 2iCs. The ways that 2iCs are unique are outlined in detail in chapters 7 and 9 of *How to be Second*.

DISCOVERING THE 2 AND 2IC

Because of the overlap in the core of "Secondness" that 2s/2iCs share, to the untrained eye, a 2 vs a 2iC occupying the same ill-fitting role may not look too much different. But in the right role, the differences visibly emerge. There are a few bright line categories where we see 2s and 2iCs diverge from one another. These categorical filters are the highest order ways of understanding the 2/2iC distinction, and there are lots of finer detail differences that fall under each category as well.

The first category is management. This refers to both the needs and style of management deployed by 2s/2iCs.

The second category, motivation, refers to energy flow—what animates and deflates a 2 vs. a 2iC?

The third category, abilities, refers to innate higher-order capabilities to do things. Abilities can manifest in applications as a host of derivative skills. If you have a general ability, specific skills for specific aligned tasks will come with relative ease compared to someone lacking the associated innate ability.

It's been funny to notice how we've read this data back into our own lives. As something in the data is illuminated, both of us would have corollary flashes of self-insight. Management, motivations, and abilities have shown up—like the data would indicate—as both similar and dissimilar between us.

In the sections that follow, you'll see how these initial categories of similarity/difference are evidenced. We move from these superordinate three categories to broad insights about differences between 2s/2iCs. Finally, we'll move into finer distinctions where 2s/2iCs converge or diverge.

Remember, these are traits and abilities that reside at an ingrained level. The differences between 2s and 2iCs are not sustainable "flexes" that the opposite type of Second can perpetually make. As such, senior leadership and hiring managers would be well-advised to, at minimum, consult the Trait Table included in chapter 7 when thinking about putting the right people in the right leadership seats.

CHAPTER 6

HOW TO BE SECOND

I set out to figure out how to be the best COO. That turned into being the best Second, which turned into being the best Second in command, which turned into being the best 2iC, which turned into being...

The best version of myself I can be.

Being Second is not about being COO.

The way to be Second is to be yourself. To own who *you* are.

That means all of your strengths and all of your weaknesses together—some of which you might be able to change, but most of which you'll only be able to adjust.

Owning that I'm going to hit my head on some things with near certainty has actually made me better at almost everything I jump into. I'm quicker to admit that I'm not the best people-person and I'm going to need help galvanizing a team. I've been quicker to own that I *get* processes in a way that other people just won't. I've learned to use my special combination of ignorance, curiosity, and perception of implication like a superpower, and I've been able to apologize *way* faster when I slip into "I'll do it myself" mode.

Perhaps the most relieving thing that anchoring to being Second has given me is a surety in my curiosity and learning. I've stopped worrying about finding a traditional niche and shifted the cornerstone of my economic value to the intersection of my self and my main interests. For me, that means being a Second in Command who is specifically interested in business. I don't feel the need to study nuclear physics "just in case" (or many, many other topics) nearly as much as I used to. I know I'm naturally built to navigate things by understanding their foundational concepts, so I've been able to focus my learning on systems instead. Specifically, business systems, but also the part that businesses play in the broader economy, and what seems positive and negative about them.

Having a place for my curiosity—and sometimes, I admit, fear of not knowing *everything*—has brought a significant amount of peace, mostly from being bought into how I can own my Secondness.

Frankly, also, it's made me a better follower. I'm a natural follower, as I believe all Seconds (of both types) are, and owning that has made me both more discerning and easier to work with. I hold much tighter to those foundations of what is good, and much more loosely to the individual parts of the puzzle. Guiding the domino line of second and third order effects has become much more fun and way less stressful.

There is definitely some thinking out there that being a Second means only being capable of playing the Right Hand and never being in the First in Command role. Or that people who are Seconds would *never* want to be a CEO, ever, and would only be followers. That just hasn't held up. It may be true that *most* people who identify as Second have no interest in that First in Command role, but what we found instead was that the inclination is not about competence, but rather seems to be all about energy and desire. We'll talk about this in more depth later, but being Second (or being anyone) means being aware of the energy drain that leading is going to place on you. Given the demands on people in that role, at least in our Western culture—well, Seconds typically don't have the energy it takes to live under those expectations all the time. It's not enjoyable or natural for us, and it definitely was not sustainable for me.

Perhaps my favorite thing about being Second and owning it that is that I've started to really showcase the things I've put my flag down in. I love playing video games, as they're a place to escape into some breathtaking pre-built systems that I can optimize with no ramifications. I love all the trappings that come along with it too, like the stories and the music and... the whole thing. During the course of writing this book, for the first time in my life, I bought some T-shirts with the logos of my absolute favorite games and developers. Because I am a fan of those things, and I'm ok with being known for that. I also wear some sick *How to be Second* branded shoes and hoodies and have the H2B2 logo sticker on my laptop, because I think this is awesome, too. I think *we* are awesome.

For the rest of the book ,we're going to really dive into the traits and tendencies of this identity, why it gets overlooked, the struggles we'll face as Seconds, and the unique struggles of 2s and 2iCs individually, because we did do a ton of research, and we feel pretty strongly about what we found. We hope you stick around for that. We feel like you'll enjoy yourself and learn something super useful.

Owning your Secondness will mean spending a stint of your life filling a bunch of different roles. Some of those roles you were basically custom built for, which is great. Own that, and let them represent you unabashedly.

But remember, you are not the role. You give just as much value to the role you're in as it gives to you.

I texted Dave one morning (as one does) to talk about the identity of being Second, and said, "Dave, I think being bought in to being a Second as part of your identity is scary. If you buy it, you're saying by proxy, 'Who I am, independently, is a person who WILL find meaning and identity in whatever group I join. I WILL be a follower and a fan, because that is the kind of human I am.' And that has terrifying implications."

And Dave, who is PhD level smart (literally) had this to say: "*Hmmmmm.*"

But then he said this:

I think what you described is the state of all identities. It's actually the point of MY writing. I think that modern people find it terrifying if they are clear-eyed about the prospect (like you are in your statement).

In the West, we have taken on the notion that we are "influence free" as part of our assumptions about being able to individually curate your own identity. The irony is that individually created identities are:

1. *never really uniquely, individually created, and*
2. *if someone holds to that notion, the corresponding identity is often fragile and needs frequent reinforcement to feel like the identity is real.*

I find it actually empowering to be clear-eyed about it. The most identity agency that we have is choosing (to the extent that we can) what group will help set and reinforce our identities.

That gets at the heart of how we're going to be Second – part of the deal is buying in.

If you're reading all this and going, "Whatever man, this isn't me," then you're probably right.

If you're thinking, "That might be mostly me but it's still not exact," you're probably *also* right. As we've said a few times, we've landed on this thing that people have been sailing around for a long time. We've planted a flag and given it a name, but we still have a lot of exploring to do,

I mean, you didn't think we'd assume we had it *all* figured out on the first shot, did you? Never mind, of course you didn't; you know us better than that by now.

Also, if you're Tony and you're like "This is *totally* me, but I don't like it!" well, forget you. (Tony, if you found this, I'll get everyone's beers next month.)

The critical part of how to be Second is the buy-in; buying into yourself, to what you choose to represent, and to being a kick-ass, discerning follower and supporter.

What is Followership?

We hold that Seconds excel at being followers, especially first followers, so now we'll deliver on that explanation we mentioned would be "coming up soon."

For better or worse, there is nothing quite as Second as followership, which we found is one of the cornerstone traits for both types of Second—and which definitely requires buy-in.

Our brains work pretty linearly most of the time. When we think of describing almost anything, we usually ask questions in this order:

- What is it?
- Why is it?
- How do we deal with it?

So, let's just run through those questions here.

What is followership is pretty straightforward. Merriam-Webster.com defines followership as "The capacity or willingness to follow a leader," which feels right—that's what we mean when talking about it.

But why does that simple description and the idea of it feel discordant? Our discomfort with following seems cultural, whether that's from the 100,000+ times we've been told we should be leaders or should want to be number one, or how often we're told not to let someone else make our decisions for us (some irony there).

Maybe it's because we associate following with social media platforms and being-famous-for-being-famous, which seems like a silly thing.

Those explanations don't feel quite complete though, because we're just as often told to look at trailblazers for inspiration, or that R&D means "rip off and duplicate" because others have done the work for us, or that mentorship is good, or to learn from others' mistakes, or even that voting is good. Which all seem like follower type activities.

So maybe culture hasn't quite made up its mind on what followership is supposed to look like.

Nathan

This confusion tracks with how I grew up, which was in a right-wing conservative home. I had to follow Jesus and my parents but question all other forms of authority, and that was very weird. It was extra weird when I started questioning Jesus AND my parents, especially because my relationship with Jesus got better with questions while my relationship with my parents got worse. Anyway, I might have started out with an extra weird perspective on followership, but that means the what, why, and how of it is something I've been sussing out for a while now.

Let's take it back to ground.

We'll leave it simple and just stick with followership as the capacity or willingness to follow a leader.

Well then, *why* is followership?

WHY IS FOLLOWERSHIP?

If followership is so easily defined as the ability to follow a leader, it begs the question, "What is a leader?" and then "Why do we have leaders?"

We think that answer is *also* simple. Perhaps frustratingly simple: We're human, and that's what we do.

We form ourselves into groups and structure those groups so there's just a few people we listen to, and we call those people leaders.

Sometimes a few people push and shove to get to the top of those groups. But sometimes random people start doing stuff all on their own that some of us think is cool, so we just form up behind them. Suddenly, those random people are "leaders" and they never even asked for it.

Even defining leaders is kind of funny to us, because the more we think about followership, the more it seems that we define leaders by talking about what traits they should possess, which are just the traits of people we would want to follow. (Or model ourselves after, which is itself a form of followership)

Actually, here's Shane Parrish and Rhiannon Beaubien from their book The Great Mental Models volume 2, explaining this better than we can:

> The interesting thing about hierarchies in humans is that their benefits aren't always obvious at first. Few people would say they like them, unless they happen to be at the top of the pile. Most of us hate having to defer to our parents, our bosses, the state...
>
> Hierarchies are inherently and inevitably unequal and unfair. Hierarchies, however, clearly confer a benefit that is large enough to balance out their costs. In the absence of an imposed structure, people have a natural instinct to self-organize. In organizations that claim to have a flat structure with no leaders, people often just end up more frazzled than normal, as they attempt to navigate the inevitable unspoken power structures

which are paramount to their success. Even anarchist movements end up with leaders. Leadership is important. Getting rid of the titles of "captain" or "boss" doesn't change the fact that someone in the locker room or the board room is going to set the example for others, so it's best to ask who we want that person to be....

...The French Revolution, with its focus on ending absolutism and subsequent return of absolute power and the rise of nationalism, can show us a lot about our hierarchical instincts. People could not destroy the hierarchy altogether; they just ended up with a new form of it.

One of the lessons here then, is that allowing for the fact of hierarchical instincts is critical in the development and leadership of any organization.

OK, if we're stuck with this happening—what do we do about it?

And how is this going to tie to Seconds being naturally good at all of this (enough to be worth taking up all these extra pages?)

All of this and more after the break.

What? There is no break? Alright then, here we go...

How Do I Deal with Followership?

"If we can't avoid hierarchies, we need to recognize their presence and focus on structuring them in the most beneficial way

for everyone involved. Like having prestige associated with be-longing to the group, rather than being conferred on individu-als. The key is, to be aware of hierarchies, and work WITH, not against them. We want to use hierarchies as a tool, not be used by them."

—Shane Parrish, Rhiannon Beaubien

In 1988, Robert Kelly wrote *"Without his armies, after all, Napoleon was just a man with grandiose ambitions."*

Without people, there is no leading to do. No hierarchy, group at all. Without people, there is no party. Just a nut, dancing alone.

And as we've seen, if we say, "We'll all join as peers," it won't last that way for long.

To get an army, or a party, or a hierarchy, or an organi-zation to work with more than one person, someone has to JOIN it. Someone has to be willing to be the first follower.

As Derek Sivers says, *"The first follower is what transforms a lone nut into a leader."*

Seconds have natural energy right in this space. Because the creativity of Seconds is most easily activated by an idea or need that others have, because they're often energized by organizing and seeing their team succeed, because they drive for a plan rather than random energy everywhere, because they typically prefer to be outside the spotlight—they are perfectly poised to be the most powerful followers in the group. Game-changing followers.

The willingness to be a follower is extraordinarily powerful. When you join something, you're at least doubling the potential that the idea you joined can become real, rather than dividing resources into two places.

If you're willing to buy into what already gives you energy, you're basically the make-or-break component of whether things work and grow or don't.

Because Seconds naturally see causes and implications, they understand that their followership means they need to be aware of what and who they say *yes* to. When you serve someone—and you're always serving *someone*—you're saying yes to what they do and say. Leaders don't build pyramids or run countries or businesses or even soup kitchens without their followers granting permission to do so.

As a follower, especially a first follower, we signal to others that what's happening is something they can be part of, or even *should* be part of. That's a form of leadership on its own.

As Seconds, we're not responsible for everything... but it can feel like it, because we understand it. That's powerful. Terrifying, but powerful.

Derek Sivers (founder of CD Baby) has a TED talk called "How to Start a Movement," wherein he drops the gem we just mentioned about the lone nut. In three minutes, he explains the crucial role of followership, and how followership is leadership. We recommend you check it out, but here's what he says about followership:

"The first follower has a crucial role, they publicly show everyone else how to follow."

"It takes guts to be a first follower because you stand out and brave ridicule yourself. The first follower is an under-appreciated form of leadership."

"It's critical for the public to see the followers, because new followers emulate followers, not the leader."

"The biggest lesson here, did you catch it? Leadership is over glorified. Yes, it started with the shirtless guy, and he'll get all the credit, but you saw what really happened: it was the first follower that transformed the lone nut into a leader."

This is about as good as it gets.

To recap, as a Second, *who you are* naturally means you're fantastic at followership. And that is something to be proud of as much or more than any other trait we possess!

Healthy vs. Unhealthy Followership

We should talk about the dark side of followership for a minute.

Followership can be healthy and unhealthy, and unhealthy followership moves toward subservience. (Being subservient vs. willing to serve.)

Subservience is *not* cool, because it doesn't wrestle with the hard parts of followership— understanding what you're supporting and constantly questioning whether it's good.

Nathan has told bosses before that he is willing to say he disagrees but commits three times in their relationship.

If the boss makes him say that more than three times, then they'll know he's not the person who can help build that thing, because he doesn't believe in what they're building.

This isn't about someone deciding what color to paint the walls (probably). It's reserved for decisions that push against his foundational beliefs. For moments that make him own his followership, when he can't simply say "yes" in good conscience.

"I was just following orders" is not something that we as Seconds need to be saying.

We want you to *own* your super powers like organizing, managing, coaching, and bringing things to life—and that includes owning it when you shouldn't be bringing that thing to life.

We've spent some time explaining the core identity markers of Seconds, and we want to do the same for the things we've heard bring or take energy for Seconds. Just "serving" is not fulfilling; there's more that goes into healthy relationships and work and sense of self than that.

So, here are some of the common things we heard that help generate energy and create that sense of fulfillment from investment:

Healthy Seconds enjoy a trusting, reciprocal relationship with a First in Command or another integral leader. In this relationship, Seconds are able to build solutions to problems and have ready access to data to make decisions and improvements. Their superior listens to potential solutions that a Second generates and ensures that the solutions have fidelity to their original vision.

In most relationships, healthy Seconds will be doing some coaching. They will work on communicating their plan well to all implicated stakeholders, and they will work to help close knowledge and skill gaps with stakeholders who need to level up to carry out a solution. Healthy Seconds seek buy-in (but not necessarily consensus) and will delicately tread the line between *proposing* solutions and *imposing* solutions. This can be true organizationally, but also in their friendships, their bands, or even their marriages.

Healthy Seconds gain some sense of security from delegating important parts of the plan upwards. Delegating up is different than managing up, as it's not so much about learning how your leaders work and how to have rapport with them as it is about trusting them to handle the things you don't have energy for. If you're focused on your team and executing the thirty-day plan, you need to be comfortable delegating the ninety-day plan up to whoever you're working with.

At first glance, delegating "your future and security" to someone else seems like putting yourself into a subservient role … but everyone is delegating their future and security to someone else, even the people at the "top" of a hierarchy. Which is why identifying the parts that don't give you energy and forming a partnership where someone else can handle them is a great idea for both parties involved.

Healthy Seconds look like a combination of a trusted aide and capable leader on their own—someone the rest of the team can rally behind and who the leaders can rely on to organize towards the goal at the same time. Followers don't emulate the leader; they emulate the other followers, and a healthy Second will teach everyone else how to harmonize together and move forward.

An unhealthy Second may have chosen to follow someone that is non-communicative. Or worse, that person makes rogue decisions as a leader that are at odds with what the Second sees as a good course of action and doesn't get on the same page with the Second to see how things do or don't line up.

Perhaps the leader keeps moving the goal post or switching the vision and is always chasing his or her next idea, even while the Second is still in the process of laying the groundwork to support the previous vision. Huge directional shifts or lack of communication, or a combination of the two, are a recipe for turning a Second towards being frustrated, hurt, judgmental, and untrusting. In essence, unsafe.

An unhealthy Second will lean into their power of insight in negative ways. Their insights become negative appraisals of people around them, and their judgment runs from being able to tease apart issues and processes to becoming personally judgmental. The Second in this situation will increasingly find themselves on a relational island, or they will begin to undermine leadership and draw people onto their side. The ability of a Second to be generative, constructive, and optimistic will erode—and the absence of these qualities is a telling mark of a Second in a bad place.

Unhealthy Seconds may have fallen into subservience, trying to support their chosen leader at all costs and attempting to delegate up their own accountability for their actions. Instead of emulating the healthiest traits of the leader and serving as a unifying force for the team, they'll act as a buffer for the leader. They'll treat the leader's toxic or ignorant behavior as brilliance beyond understanding, or they'll ignore its lack of substance and vilify people who don't conform.

How Rare Is Being a Second?

Seconds are pretty rare. Even before the added nuance of 2s and 2iCs, only 2 percent or less of the population were naturally "this way," according to Mark Winters and Gino Wickman in their books *Rocket Fuel* and *Traction*, respectively. With the nuance of 2s and 2iCs added, each of those would be even more rare, overall.

But now that we've focused on the identity and not the role, and added the nuance of the split identities underneath the umbrella of "Secondness," we've actually had a lot *more* people self-identify or buy into being this thing. We can only go by our guts and our research so far—which means a sample size of more than hundreds but less than thousands— but we believe the number of Seconds in the population is actually a bit higher than that 2 percent.

We also hope that getting this book published will help us increase our sample size dramatically, for a more accurate headcount.

What we believe to be true based on our data so far is that about 4 percent of the population is naturally a Second. Or, 1 of every random sampling of 25 people.

We believe that you'll find a few Seconds of either type naturally clustered in almost any established group of 25 people, and probably at least 1 within the first 5-7 people on most teams. Basically, to reiterate some of the natural tendencies, both types of Seconds are attracted to teams.

We also believe that certain types of teams tend to attract or repel 2s and 2iCs uniquely, so it's possible to be *less* random in your sampling.

Seconds are attracted to teams and hierarchies as part of who they are, and teams built on cultures that celebrate "servanthood" as a moral good attract all Seconds like a magnet.

For every 100 people that gather in churches or other places of faith, we'd expect to find 15 percent or more of the community who would identify as a type of Second, most likely 2s. You're likely to find that 80 percent of the church "leadership team" in an evangelical setting would identify as 2s, and there's probably another half-dozen of them in the Kid's Church and Cafe.

On the flipside, fast growth startups might see no Seconds of either kind in their first 30-50 people. If these cultures did attract a Second, they'd be much more likely to attract a 2iC and perhaps even repel 2s. Workwise, they seem like they'd attract people who love to be generalists, but the purpose of the group tends to be inherently competitive, with most of the focus being necessarily on the work and extreme pace, often at the cost of team health. Not a place 2s tend to like.

You're more likely to find 2s spending time in established teams. Either very large teams, or very small and old organizations that won't ever get any bigger and seem like kind of a mess. It's just more comfortable in those spaces, and there's more obvious value placed on the natural tendencies of 2s.

Meanwhile, 2iCs would be likely to revolt upon setting foot in the door of most places like that.

Larger organizations seem to be especially attractive to 2iCs because there are lots of positions that aren't Second in Command but still provide an incredibly broad locus of control with comparatively little oversight. General Managers or Division Managers of Fortune 5000 companies seem to self-identify more than usual when Nathan speaks on the topic of Seconds—specifically, the identity markers of 2iCs—in rooms of executives.

So, Seconds overall aren't super rare purple unicorns like some people tend to think, but they are sort of hidden and tend to congregate into certain spots. It's easy to see why they're *perceived* as super rare in the business world, especially certain parts of the business world. Not every Second (of either type) is necessarily interested in business, and when you've sliced the pie that many times, they probably are super rare in any given niche.

Also, 2s and 2iCs are different, and 2iCs do seem to be much rarer overall.

Which kind of feels like a good thing for everyone.

Can You Become a Second?

Basically, no. You can't become a Second any more than you can change how you were born.

The question is not whether or not someone in your company can fill the responsibilities and role of a Second in Command or manager-type person. That is entirely possible (and probable). This role is of such importance that it cannot be abandoned for the lack of an available 2/2iC. However, we've all seen what a difference it makes when the right person occupies the right seat in an organization. What was a role becomes an expanding capacity with synergistic imagination—suddenly integration, planning, and processes can transform with ease. People up and down the reporting chain have a different experience of the role by the identity of the person in the seat.

Someone who has the innate tendencies of a Second can be more than a release valve for the administrative requirements that allow the organizational machine to run. In fact, organizational performance will improve when a Second of either type occupies the role that beckons someone of their composition and skill.

The question of a Second vs. not in a role is one of outside-in vs inside out. A Contributor who is not a Second will work from the externally identified needs and duties allocated to a role. The Contributor may be able to figure out how to satisfice (to make do instead of something truly satisfactory), to keep the administrative items in their realm from malfunctioning—and we are not knocking this. Any Contributor might be able to use a checklist generated by a Second to simulate the shell of a process, and you might be able to "eat the list," internalize it, and become a Second with limited creativity in a specific domain or role. This will keep things from breaking down.

But the difference between a non-Second and a natural Second in a role is that a non-Second can only renovate and repair an existing process or system—they will not be as capable of innovation as a natural Second. Their ability to follow a checklist or process would not easily transfer across domains in a way that any Contributor could come up with an equivalent process or checklist in a new domain. If you are a natural second, the innate qualities of that identity will allow you transfer these generative qualities to new situations and areas of performance.

In short... can you become a 2/2iC? No, not even if you step into their shoes. A natural Second will have the internal orientation (and sensibilities to seek tools) to augment, support, externalize, and amplify the thinking patterns, attentional foci, and strategies that we recognize in a Second. A non-Second typically will not. If you currently have a Contributor or Artisan in a role that demands a Second, you don't know what you don't know regarding what that role could actually accomplish.

CHAPTER 7

AM I A SECOND? WHICH ONE?

HOLD TIGHT, the next couple pages are a huge caveat. Yes, we felt we had to do this.

There's an old parable about blind people finding an elephant.

Basically, a group of blind people have never been around an elephant before, and then one day, they come across one.

Together, they try to learn what the thing they came across is by touching it (because they're blind), and then they describe it to each other based on the bit that they got a hand on.

Of course, they each get a hand on some wildly different bit of the elephant. Someone touches a tail, another a tusk, another a leg, etc., and each of them describes the whole elephant as being only the bit they found. Then they argue about it, because each of them is both correct and incorrect.

Depending on where you get your version of the story from, the basic points are:

1. Almost nobody can get the whole picture of something by themselves.
2. Stuff can be two things.
3. It's not that you're wrong, you're just not *all* right.

And that leads us to finding yourself and personality assessments. How? Because most personality assessments measure some part of you, and they can feel incredibly accurate... but we like to refer to them as "one hand on the elephant."

Personality tests are blindly putting hands on something and telling you what it's like. They aren't necessarily wrong, they're just not *all* right.

The tempting thing to do is take one and let it guide you as best it can. This is especially tempting if you find you're one of the "rare" ones. You might proudly say:

- "I'm an (four letters)."
- "I'm a (five strengths)."
- "I'm a (number/wing)."
- "I'm a (color)."

But you probably have strengths *and* a number/wing *and* four letters *and* some colors *and* a high "S" *and* you're an intro/extro/ambivert *and*...

Because stuff can be two things. (Or twenty things. Or a hundred things.)

People are big, messy, complicated, woobily shapes built out of a lot of similar building blocks. That means we can get constructs like introverts and extraverts, or 2s and 2iCs, or whatever types of boxes we have for things that seem to behave in a consistent way, because sometimes people are put together with similar building blocks, in similar ways. Humans also like to simplify things, so if they have a box they'll see if you can fit in it. If you fit, even poorly, they'll label you as that thing and call it a day. We'll even do that to ourselves. Paradoxically, humans also like to be individuals, so they also fight against being labeled, even by themselves... except we also want to be in community... and the fact that we like to have an identity... It's all a total cluster.

The point is, we're complicated.

(Including you, person who read all that and still went, "Well, except me, I'm pretty simple.")

If you're still on track, the *next* point is that no one can get the whole picture of something by themselves. (Including us.)

We interviewed a *lot* of people over almost two years and asked them a *lot* of questions about Seconds, including what their personality tests said or didn't say.

And by that, we mean we found as many blind people as we could and had them all touch an elephant, identified the most consistent things they said, and decided that's what we're going to talk about.

So can you actually, "safely" self-identify as a Second, or as a 2 or 2iC, based on reading this book? We think we've done as good a job as anyone of getting this box shaped as closely as possible to what we think will fit, and we want to give you the best possible opportunity to make the attempt.

But at the end of the day, you're a woobily shape, so we just don't freaking *know*, y'know?

As you continue through these descriptions, we invite you to email us with your thoughts about what fits and doesn't.

How 2s and 2iCs Are Different

I hope you're ready for a bunch of ways that Seconds break down into the unique identities of 2s and 2iCs.

Vernacular for this section is going to be difficult. We're going to be using terms like Second and 2s and 2iCs and maybe some other numbers and role markers like Second in Command and First in Command and Right Hand, all in really close proximity.

Forgive us, the jumble of it all has been the issue, so here's a quick reminder of how we're pulling apart the mess:

- Second is the umbrella term. When we say "Second" or "all Seconds" we mean the entire group of Seconds, comprised of both 2s and 2iCs.
- When we say 2s, we mean specifically people who identify as 2s.
- When we say 2iCs, we mean specifically people who identify as 2iCs.
- When we say First in Command, we mean the role of first in command (which anyone can hold).
- When we say Second in Command, we mean the role of being Second in Command (which anyone can hold).

Finally, when we say 1iC we mean this *other* personality—a person that we don't want to talk about much, but it can't be helped. When we say 1iC, we mean that person who is "naturally suited to the First in Command role," in the same way that Seconds seem to fit into the Second in Command spot. When people use "Visionary" as a trait and not a role, they mean this person. Sorry.

Oh, and when we say "That's quite confusing," we mean exactly that.

OK, here we go!

WHEN DO YOU SEE?

When we're asking this question, we're just asking about *when* your thoughts tend to settle. Where do your thoughts tend to focus as you move through your day and your activities? Do you tend to find what's happening In the right now Important? Do you tend to focus on the things that aren't quite here yet but you can see being real? Or maybe you think In the far flung future? Let's plot it out a little, shall we?

Time

Minutes > Hours > Days > Weeks > Months > Seasons >
A Year > Some Years > Eventually

Importance

Critical > Important > Normal > Unimportant > Forgettable

Can you draw lines between the two groups about where you tend to find yourself focusing?

Obviously, everyone needs to be conscious on some level about what's happening right in front of them, but is what's happening in these next few minutes unimportant unless it touches something you're trying to move that's months away? Perhaps whatever Is going to happen a season or two from now Is forgettable to you, and what's happening today Is critical, It's all that matters?

Our "When do you see?" theory posits that different types of people naturally think in different time horizons, or find the activities within those time horizons to be the most important activities to them. We'll focus on comparing Seconds of both types, with some references to that 1iC type sprinkled in as well. We've tried to avoid talking about the 1iC personality type as much as possible, but it sort of can't be helped.

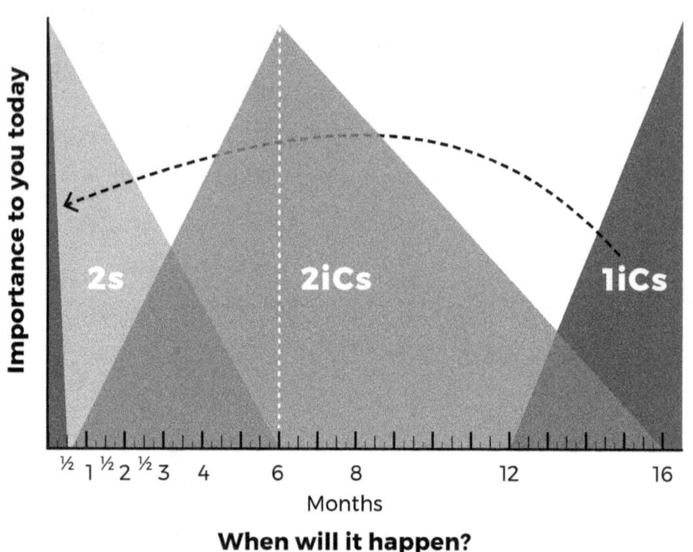

When will it happen?

The average person seems to spend most of their time placing Importance on what will happen In the next few minutes out to a few weeks from now, and further out things can get a bit hazy and unimportant. With effort, it's totally possible to move that focus out further, but it's not where things tend to settle. Seconds tend to see a little further out, with just a couple of distinctions: 2s tend to mentally live between days and seasons as their Important and critical points, where 2iCs tend to live in the month to a year area.

Neither type of Second seems to have a high amount of energy for seeing the detail in the immediate, whatever we're doing to get through this week Is forgettable unless It touches what they're trying to bring Into reality over the next three to six months. Long stretches of being "in the weeds" or considering the situations of today as critical, wears on a Second.

2s seem to be fine stretching their thinking out to seasons or a year, but it bumps against feelings of disconnect from reality, as they naturally place Importance closer to the Immediate.

2iCs tend to live in the month to a year area. Thinking in weeks is fine, but considering the day can be difficult or feel pointless. Similar feelings pop up when going out past the year mark—eventually, things just feel like a dream, and you can only make tangible decisions with real effects that you can measure in shorter terms. So sure, stretch out for the multi-year idea, but let's talk about what we're going to do *this* year to make that happen, that's what's Important.

Finally, the 1iC person tends to live in the micro-micro of minutes and hours, *and also* at the polar opposite end, way out at "eventually," with a gigantic blind spot in between. It's as if 1iCs have microscopic attention to detail when they're doing the work they're focused on, while keeping the three-year picture or even the "eventually" picture in their head, with almost no feelings of Importance for what sits between those two.

BIG CAVEAT: We're not here to weigh in on whether short – or long-term thinking is better. The answer is probably "it depends." And we're not saying that your time horizon is set in stone; you can probably train yourself to see the details or to appreciate the multi-year picture.

Here, we're focusing on what we've seen hold steady again and again across all kinds of people, and this "when they see" theory seems to hold some water.

During some coaching sessions, the phrase "Domino Theory" was coined, which relates directly to the "When do you see" theory. Effectively, seeing effects or implications in progressive order, like a waterfall. This is also directly related to "First and Second Order" thinking. There are nuances on all sides, but the concepts seem to overlap heavily on each other.

Risk Tolerance

All Seconds seem to be naturally more risk averse, but 2s seem to lean more heavily into that tendency, whereas 2iCs seem to have a much higher tolerance or capacity for risk.

We believe this is either because of the intersection of several of their other natural traits, or that it's the jumping off point for those traits.

Having a slightly longer time horizon, thinking in multiple order effects, and caring for people in a more structural than personal way, means 2iCs are not only willing to have a conversation about doing something that seems risky, they're likely willing to lead the charge.

That being said, when you find a 2iC leading the charge, you can probably guess that there's some guiding principle at work. Likely, the undertaking itself has some strong value, without any kind of "long-term vision" necessary. The immediate work they're leading the charge on is valuable for the sake of itself, or the benefit is clear in the short-term.

Honestly, this book is a good example. We know the book itself is valuable. The effect it will have on people's lives has already borne out in text messages, interview commentary, emails sitting in our inboxes, and conversations in coffee shops. People have already felt *seen*, have new language to use in conversations with loved ones, and have connected to great jobs.

But when people ask us what the three-year or five – or ten-year outlay is for the work of How to be Second, we shrug. We know it's valuable, but there is no "big vision" or "future state" that we're necessarily trying to bring into the world.

We've both started businesses and now work in jobs that we're overall happy about. We like the independence of running our own things, but prefer the stability and collaborative position that comes with being on a team. Even the work of the book is something we tackled collaboratively, and we carried the risks of the endeavor largely inside our natural tendencies of Nathan being a 2iC, and David being a 2 (we believe).

Remember the Derek Sivers video we talked about in chapter 6? It focuses on the first person who jumps into the dance, saying that "the person who started it is seen as the leader, and they'll get all the credit, but it's really the first follower who turned the lone nut into a leader."

Both types of Seconds are likely to be that first follower, but the 2iC specifically seems more willing to be the Lone Nut.

It's not about whether you have the **competence** to be the leader, the starter, the entrepreneur, or the lone nut. It's about whether you have the **energy** to do so, and keep at it.

Caring for People Looks Like "Not Caring"

Those who are Seconds seem to have a built-in high capacity for managing teams. While 2s tend to care for their teams on a more personal level, 2iCs tend to care for their teams on a structural level.

If a team member is acting poorly or not performing to the standard, 2s might immediately think about what could be done to care for that person and bring them back into function with the team. A 2iC's first thought would be to cut the person from the team.

To the 2iC, this isn't callous; it *is* their version of care. They see issues with people as structural. Someone "not cutting it" might mean a limited resource pool for time off is going to be distributed so that each person on the team has plenty, while giving extra consideration to one person might throw the entire team out of alignment over the long-term.

The 2iC considers the moral dilemma of the Trolley Problem and says, "This entire situation is awful, but I'm pretty sure we should pull the lever for the single person track. And I will do it."

It smacks of catastrophizing and callousness and almost paints the 2iC in a villainous shade. And sometimes, that might not feel far off. Though most daily situations don't carry ethical consequences that are quite so severe, decisions that affect people in dramatic ways *are* common, and few people can see them (or are willing to see them) like the 2iC can.

Again, this *is* the way they care. The phrase "Utilitarian Empathy" popped up during our conversations as an attempt to explain the way that 2iCs have empathy and attempt to share that through utilitarian choices made on behalf of their teams. They can actually box up and use the *idea* of empathy itself as a tool to further the structural needs of their teams.

All 2iCs have to smack against this wall of seeming callousness at some point. If they want to continue to grow as people, they'll have to lean into caring for individuals on a personal level somehow. Usually, that means finding some 2s to work with. But it doesn't mean giving up the ability to see objectively and make those decisions.

Side by Side Trait Comparison Table

Steve Price, a friend of Nathan's, suggested we create a side-by-side table to help showcase the differences between 2s and 2iCs. This felt a bit like walking into a streetlight—it made us feel ridiculous for not having seen it even as it smacked us in the face.

We reviewed our data (again) and outlined ninety unique points that seemed to get highlighted in either their similarities or differences when 2s or 2iCs were answering questions or being spoken of. We took those ninety points and grouped them into four broad categories: management, motivation, self, and abilities.

We discussed the Self category earlier. We've discussed some of the others throughout the book as well, like the commonalities of willingness to be the first follower, needing a plan, and being more generalist in skillset. We've also just pointed out a few of the diverging points, like 2iCs tending to have a higher risk tolerance, and later we'll see more, such as 2s tending to be better player coaches.

We feel that it's important enough to warrant reminder that the core between both 2s and 2iCs is similar, with divergence on the fringes.

Quick image for reference, and onto the comparison table!

Trait Overlap

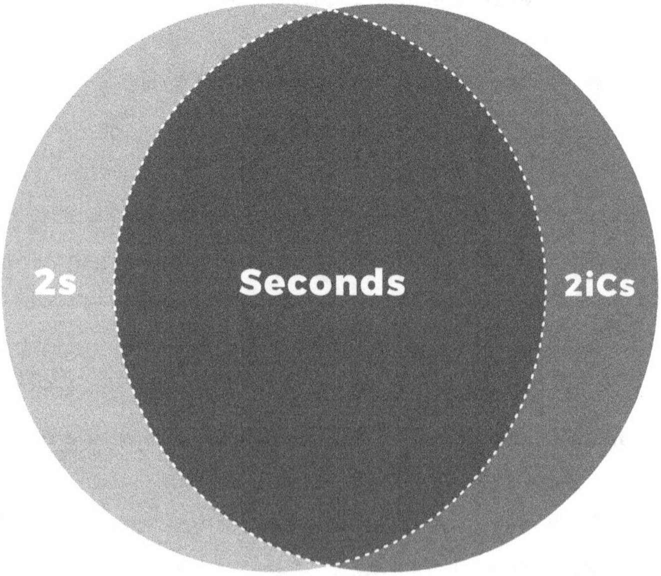

MANAGEMENT

Tendency	2s	2iCs
Often find themselves in charge of teams	Yes	Yes
Gets energy from coaching the team	Yes	Rarely
Gets energy from managing the system for the team	Rarely	Yes
Judges people on "perceived" competence	Rarely	Often
Easy to perceive people as roadblocks	Rarely	Often
Able to be convinced with feelings	Often	Rarely
Willing to fight their superiors	Rarely	Often
Willing to say "no" to superiors	Sometimes	Often
Willing to say "yes" even when unsure	Yes	Rarely
Tends to find themselves on relational islands	Rarely	Often
Tends to be team-focused	Yes	Yes
People naturally turn to them for support, whether emotional or skill-based	Yes	No
Enablers of poor habits, may allow toxic behavior for extended periods of time	Yes	Rarely
Contorts themselves to make peace	Yes	Rarely
Focuses on others, gets people unstuck, makes people feel welcomed	Yes	Rarely

Struggles to say "no" when given assignments	Yes	No
Tends to naturally align themselves into a follower position	Yes	No
Gets stuck in hierarchy (asks their own boss, but not their boss's boss)	Yes	No
Accused of "not caring" for people	Rarely	Often
Can be seen as the villain	Rarely	Often
Willing to let people go from the team	Rarely	Often
Relationships vs Systems	Tends to build relationships and finds systems	Tends to build systems and finds relationships
Intimidating to others	Rarely	Often
Leading individual contributors	Excels	Struggles
Leading leaders	Struggles	Excels
Requires the ability to adjust the system	Sometimes	Always

MOTIVATION

Tendency	2s	2iCs
Activated by a spark of vision from another person	Yes	Yes
Best when partnering with a strong leader with mutual respect	Yes	Yes

Confidence often comes from the perspective of others	Yes	Yes
NEED to feel "competent"	Yes	Yes
NEED to prepare; learn to feel competent	Yes	Crippling
Struggles with Imposter Syndrome	Significant	Crippling
Need a plan to have confidence moving forward	Yes	Yes
Slower to be convinced	Yes	Yes
Introverted	Can be	Can be
Extroverted	Can be	Can be
Prefers to be outside of the spotlight	Yes	Yes
Celebrates wins	Often	Rarely
Slower to start	Often	Often
Willing to go alone	Eventually	Yes
Tends to start work with people or processes	People	Processes
Tends to have a high willingness to serve	Yes	Yes
Appreciates Hierarchy	Yes	To split work
Tends to be collaborative rather than competitive	Yes	Yes
Have a lot of energy to give to others and get a lot of energy from seeing other people excel	Yes	No
Have a lot of energy to give on behalf of others, get a lot of energy from seeing the system work	No	Yes

Dedicated to people as the highest priority, and "the group cause" itself as a much lower priority	Yes	No
Naturally driven to rise through the ranks	Sometimes	Yes
Tends to move from pursuit to pursuit	Crippling	Sometimes
Lower "ego"	Yes	No
Tends to find their sense of self-worth in the value that others receive from them	Yes	No
Driven to excellence	Yes	Yes
Less need to design the plan than to HAVE a plan	Yes	No
Tempted to the position of First in Command because of the "power"	Rarely	Sometimes
Tempted to the position of First in Command because of control of the system	Rarely	Often
Outsized ego and drive	Rarely	Often
Likely to desire movement to the First in Command seat	Rarely	Rarely

ABILITIES

Tendency	2s	2iCs
Naturally competent	Yes	Yes
High bar for "competence"	Yes	Crippling
Naturally sees or senses causes and implications	Yes	Yes

Processes ideas in Implications (second order thinking)	Yes	Crippling
Attempts to put details and plans around "big ideas"	Yes	Always
Can see what's there and what's missing (not either/or)	Yes	Crippling
Tends to build processes	Often	Always
Tends to build processes at enterprise level	Rarely	Always
Gets energy from being on the team as a contributor	Often	Rarely
Tends to naturally externalize systems to think over them	Yes	Yes
Tends to have a generalist skillset	Yes	Yes
Future Sight? (When do you see?)	Slightly shorter term— weeks to months	Slightly longer term— months to a year+
Very high built-in capacity for being managers of teams.	Yes	No
Tends to have high natural empathy	Yes	No
Might describe their behavior with the phrase "Utilitarian Empathy"	No	Yes
Excellent Player Coaches	Yes	Rarely
Competent to be or "CEO" or "First in Command"	Usually	Yes
Builds deep expertise in a skillset	Rarely	Often
High level of curiosity	Yes	Yes

Quickly competent at new endeavors	Yes	Yes
Struggles with specialization	Often	Sometimes
Energy for creating the plan	Takes a lot	Gives a lot
Risk tolerance : willing to be the first follower?	High	High
Risk tolerance: willing to be the lone nut?	Low	High
Solves issues	In the present, when people are hurt	In the future, so people won't get hurt
Develops complex, interconnected systems	Rarely	Often

WOW, that was so much. We'll probably also make this available on our website, *howtobesecond.com*.

Traits of 2s and 2iCs in detail

Now that we've started to untangle the mess, we're going to really unpack the traits we've found here in detail to see if you can find yourself on one side of the coin more cleanly.

Don't forget these two things:

1. *You may not be this thing at all,* and you shouldn't feel bad about that.
2. You may be one of these *people* but sit in a *role* that "doesn't fit"—think about yourself as you read, rather than your role.

During Nathan's interview with Kristie Clayton, she asked, *"Who do you want me to be, the Integrator of BCR OR the Visionary of FIM?"* and he had to stop and clarify, *"Kristie. I want you to be Kristie, the person."*

2s Tend to be People-Focused for Their Teams

2s seem to have a very high built-in capacity for being managers of teams.

Specifically, they tend to be collaborative rather than competitive, and have a higher natural ability for empathy with others. They tend to find themselves in positions of leadership or team management, even without the title, and people naturally turn to them for support, whether emotional – or skill-based.

2s will often rise to management positions, and it's not uncommon to see them in "Head of" positions or VP roles. It's equally or more common to see them passed over for those positions while someone with more skill-based expertise is promoted, then the 2 ends up helping the new VP actually do the team leadership component of their job.

This stings when it happens, especially in a Western culture where the push is to rise through the ranks as a means of finding self-worth and progression. However, the 2 is thinking about the needs of their team. So while it can be frustrating to be passed over, they'll likely soon be distracted by taking care of the team and their new boss.

2s have a lot of energy to give to others and receive a lot of energy from seeing other people excel. They are generally dedicated to people as the highest priority, with "the group cause" itself having a much lower priority. That energy is present regardless of whether it's the people they manage or people they just support.

At best, 2s are the greatest player coaches among us. They are simultaneously interested in filling whatever spot the team needs the most at the time, doing so with almost alarming competence across a huge variety of skill sets, and also making sure that the people around them get what they need to perform well.

At worst, 2s are enablers of poor habits. They can allow toxic behavior to go on way too long, contorting themselves to peace-make between terrible bosses or toxic Contributors and the rest of the team. Instead of helping people grow, they simply help people not implode on themselves (and thus experience the true cost of their actions), the pain of which is oftentimes the needed ingredient to galvanize change.

2iCs Tend to be Systems-Focused for Their Teams

2iCs tend to care for people more structurally and may struggle to lead individual contributors. They tend to have a lot of energy to invest in listening to people, asking questions, and learning, and they get a lot of energy from seeing the team succeed through a well-built system. 2iCs will tend to give praise toward processes and less toward people, or they'll lead team members by explaining fundamentals rather than focusing on that person's specific contributions.

2iCs care deeply for their teams and rarely blame people, pointing first at processes to cast blame. However, the way they show care tends to be focused on adjusting the structure for the team, which is something most people can't feel. If you're on a 2iC's team, it can often feel like you haven't even been heard. You *have* been heard, loud and clear, but because the 2iC is doing something that will affect the system, the actual changes being made won't touch you directly until days, weeks, or months later. Team members can feel in a lurch in the near term.

If you're more familiar with leadership roles and managing bigger, slower moving things, you're more likely to see how much the 2iC is working on behalf of their team, and you'll find some camaraderie there. *Beware,* though: if you're in a leadership role, the 2iC will expect you to be highly competent about your part of the system. While the 2iC typically hesitates to cast blame on individual contributors for the failure of the team overall, they *will* cast blame on you for not having improved your part of the system.

2s Are More Generalist in Skillset

All Seconds tend to be generalists rather than specializing in an area.

That isn't to say that they might not be competent enough to be a CEO, or a great Artist, or a Head of Finance, or a Doctor—which are all things that require an incredible amount of study and dedication. It's to say that they're unlikely to be the "greatest" in whatever niche they find themselves in.

The natural curiosity of all Seconds means being constantly pulled from focusing on one thing at the expense of other things. When they dive into any circle of knowledge, they notice the other circles of knowledge touching the one they're in, and the spark to explore is lit again.

Combine that with a natural aptitude for almost any work (curiosity is very helpful for that) and they'll not only be drawn to explore many things, but they'll be pretty good at all of them pretty quickly. This means the skillset of Seconds will likely end up being almost weirdly broad with appreciable competence in a lot of things.

As 2s specifically tend to be more team focused than mission focused, as well as naturally curious, they're likely to jump into learning a lot of different things to support the people around them.

The struggle we've seen for 2s comes when they kick against this, for whatever reason. Societal pressures or team pressures may cause 2s to feel like they need to truly specialize, which will be very difficult for them. This means 2s will feel like other people around them are "smarter" than themselves in specific things, and the 2s will be torn between their struggle with feeling competent and their desire to celebrate the achievements of those around them. This tends to manifest in 2s as a self-driving dissatisfaction rather than an outward competitiveness.

In the business conversation about needing to fill the role of COO or a Second in Command, for a business, it's easy to elevate 2s to the position (or find that they're already there by accident). This curiosity and broad skillset is one of the critical base components that the role begs for.

2iCs Tend to Develop at Least One Area of Deep Expertise

While all Seconds tend to be above average generalists, 2iCs tend to develop deep skillsets in a few particular areas they find fascinating or useful. Most 2iCs we interviewed who were in professional roles usually doubled up as a general leader and a specialist in a particular field. In the Second in Command podcast by Cameron Herold, where he interviews almost exclusively COOs, the same is usually true of his guests.

Whatever other focused skills they choose, almost all 2iCs seem to have a natural ability to create systems, however that manifests itself. If you're a rally car co-driver, inventing a brand new system for taking and reading course notes that goes on to become the standard for co-drivers everywhere doesn't seem like a stretch. If you're a 2iC who specializes in business development for nonprofits, you'll probably develop the best system that exists on how to dependably bring in grant and donation dollars.

That's all assuming that you can get that 2iC to actually *show* those systems to anyone. Often, 2iCs create whole systems for things just to understand them, and even if they're the best in class for what they are, they just end up in some forgotten spreadsheet or notebook somewhere.

Future Sight between 2s and 2iCs

We've developed a graph that we believe will be helpful to refer to for this section. Refer back to page 104 to see it.

All Seconds, both 2s and 2iCs, tend to perceive the "bigger picture" of how things are than most Contributors. Said differently, they see further out on the time horizon. We recognize that this is a capacity that can be improved quite a bit with training and experience no matter who you are, and as far as we can tell, everyone's time horizon shortens under stress.

Also as far as we can tell, 2s seem to naturally focus between *right-now-this-very-moment*, out to a month or two in the future. We've touched on this already.

While all Seconds tend to think in multiple order effects pretty naturally, 2s may struggle to spend time reflecting on multiple-order effects unless they're anchored to a person they care about.

The energy it takes to look out much further than a month or two or to think through multiple order effects can leave 2s exhausted. It can feel like you're not focused on what's happening around you now, including what your team is doing day to day and towards their futures, which is what feels important.

That means 2s tend to make *excellent* Right Hands to their leaders, but it also means that they can struggle to keep up when expected to be a thought partner to a First in Command or 2iC. 2s can make excellent CEOs or firsts in command for a similar reason, as they're most likely to create a team-focused environment and provide a helping hand rather than a firm hand to their team members. They can struggle as Firsts in Command for the exact same reasons.

2iCs seem to naturally live further out in the time horizon, somewhere between a month or a few years. Multiple order effects are the bread and butter of 2iCs, as they see things that are happening in the right now in the ways that they're linked to the greater system. Like seeing individual actions as the center of concentric circles of effects.

2iCs will often act as a bridge between First in Commands and 2s, or in a more business sense, between CEOs and Managers, translating the larger *why* and *what* into a digestible blow-by-blow process that 2s can then lead their teams inside of. This is regularly a core requirement of COO of Chief of Staff job descriptions.

2iCs, by proxy of their further-out perception and multiple order thinking, will often end up gathering their own followings. They'll attract people who take comfort in their ability to see the "reality" of the situation and act in practical terms. They're likely to be told that they'd be excellent business owners or that everything would run better if they were in charge.

2iCs can also make excellent CEOs or First in Commands because of their far sight and ability to provide their teams rails to execute on. They can struggle because of their ability to see the multiple order effects as it manifests into the weight of understanding the actual work involved to get to that future state and the energy drain of that. Sometimes they can be paralyzed in making a decision, trying to gather up all of the information they feel like they need before making a move—a move they see as a massive shift, when the people around them see the entire situation as a throwaway decision.

High Willingness to Serve

While all Seconds attempt to care for their teams, 2s will move quickly to start caring personally for a teammate that has a need. Whether they address the need directly or attempt to adjust things within their sphere of influence, this will likely become their primary drive until they see the issue improve or absorbed into the primary mission by leadership. As mentioned already, this willingness to serve also means that 2s are easily pulled in a lot of different directions—both mentally and skillset-wise.

2s tend to have a fairly low ceiling on their own egos. While other people are making self-focused political moves, 2s tend to stay focused on being supportive and moving things forward for everyone. Even when asked to do things that seem to be either below their station or a stretch for their current skillset.

2s see things that others might perceive as slights as just par for the course. *Someone* has to do it, and they *can*, so... sure, they will. Also, they probably were curious about doing that anyway, and it's a good excuse to read that book/buy that thing anyway. *And* maybe they could find a way to make it better too, so it's actually a great opportunity!

Seconds in general tend to find their sense of self-worth in the value that others receive from them, and 2s seem to more strongly than 2iCs. (*Yup, that simple statement might sting. We wish it didn't.*) Being willing to do what other people aren't interested in doing is an EASY way for 2s to know they're going to be valued. 2s will wait to raise their hand until no one else does, but once no one else does, that hand is going up. The group needs a CEO and nobody volunteered? Their hand will go up, because that's what the team needs to move forward. The group needs a dishwasher and no one volunteered? Their hand goes up, because that's what the team needs to move forward. The group needs a CEO on Monday and dishwasher on Tuesday? Yup, their hand probably goes up.

This might come off like 2s aren't driven to excellence, but that would be incorrect. We would argue that it means they have *more* reasons to be driven to excellence. Natural curiosity, the awareness of others, the drive to support others, and having some self-worth tied up in all of that, translates to an incredible drive for high-level performance.

The difference in that performance is typically that feelings of success for 2s will come from their team being in good shape, rather than achieving personal certifications, acclamation, or positions.

2iCs Have a High Willingness to Serve, but are Quickly Willing to Take Power

2iCs regularly just want something to *be*, and when they can't find it, they're willing to build it themselves or take charge of the current group just to make sure that specific part of the world exists and works.

Largely to do with their willingness to address things they see as broken in some way, 2iCs will continue to push upward in scope of control until they've reached as high as needed to effect the change they're looking for.

It usually has nothing to do with the ego typically associated with "being in power"; it's more about the ability to make the changes they see as necessary. Once they're latched on to something being important, they'll do and learn whatever is necessary to reach a point where they can affect that change.

Interestingly, this means 2iCs are likely to see many people's personal endeavors as somewhat unnecessary. The 2iC might point to another group who is already doing that thing in what seems like a totally satisfying way, and wonder why anyone would build a new thing instead of just joining the thing that already works.

If a 2iC feels like they won't be heard but they've decided that the mission or system in question *should* exist, they're much more likely to just build something themselves (and become a First in Command) than spending any more energy changing everyone else's mind from the inside.

And again, *competence is not the same as energy.* The role of the First in Command in human hierarchies seems to beg for whoever is filling it to have a certain set of skills, and 2iCs generally have those skills. What they typically do not have is the energy that it takes to live each day using those particular skills.

We'd bet good money that some of the strongest CEOs in the world are comparatively incompetent to most business-trained 2iCs when it comes to technical expertise in finance, operations, sales, marketing, and how it all works together. But the First in Command seat is rarely about being individually, technically competent, and 2iCs generally prefer that first follower role.

2s and 2iCs and the Tendency to Go Alone or Together

You know the saying if you want to go fast, go alone, and if you want to go far, go together? 2s tend to go together, whether that's paired up with someone they trust or embedded within a team. Because of their tendency to go together and be helpful, 2s end up with a lot of mentors and people who pour into them. They're generally receptive and interested, and these relationships can go far or turn into solid friendships.

2s like knowing that *someone* has a plan for *how* to get whatever is being done, done. 2s also generally prefer to receive that plan or to collaborate to generate one. Typically in healthy 2s, this is a basic test of their leader's competence and an easy way to be part of what's going on.

2iCs tend to go alone, including struggling with looking to others for guidance. 2iCs are still voraciously curious, so they might have two or three coaches at a time, but they're probably working on specific things that they've already decided on their own are growth points to focus on.

2iCs seem to paint the structural picture of how things should be in their heads, and then seek out specific guidance as they get stuck along the way.

They tend to put in the research ahead of time, so when it's time to look for help, they're pretty exact about what they want. In the early stages of trying to determine what the plan itself is, it's just easier to be alone until it gets figured out.

Nathan

If you're a 2iC type, you *want* an instruction manual; you want that clarity. You'll also nitpick it to death, assume 80 percent of it is stuff you know already, and dismiss it out of hand. Oh, and then later when you come across something that would have been super helpful earlier, you'll get upset that no one told you until then.

2iCs Tend to be Loyal to People Rather Than Processes

As much as 2iCs focus on structures and systems, they're actually incredibly loyal to people, not processes. An unhealthy 2iC might be rabid about the process, but the healthier a 2iC is, the more they see processes as tools to achieve an outcome. They become willing to shape those processes for the sake of the people inside of them—especially to accomplish the big vision of their First in Command counterpart, if they have one.

Performances are a referendum on the utility of processes and systems, and a successful performance is a demonstration of processes working efficiently and seamlessly. In essence, most 2iCs are likely to skip the afterparty, or if they go, they'll be talking or thinking about how to improve things for next time.

2iCs Will Move the World to Work for Them

Some people might learn to live within their sphere of influence and just deal with the processes in their lives, even when they seem a bit broken.

2s will probably move to tidy up their sphere, addressing some of those processes, including pushing things up a level of authority. 2iCs will encounter an annoyance in a process and go up as high in the entire system as necessary to address the fundamental issue. There is no such thing as something outside their sphere of influence—only what's outside their sphere of attention.

A 2iC might have a perfectly organized closet and then one day decide that something about it annoys them. They'll probably have a good idea of what's bothering them and address that specific thing, and to be fair, sometimes that means re-organizing the entire closet. Addressing a cultural issue within a trillion-dollar market segment is not any more or less out of reach than re-organizing the closet. It's just that the 2iC might not care.

2iCs Have Seemingly Worse Mental Health

2iCs seem to commonly struggle with a combination of imposter syndrome and brilliance that culminates in a weird humility that feels like condescension to others.

Especially difficult is when a 2iC has to sort of choose their own destiny or purpose. The ennui can be crippling, watching a 2iC cast about from one endeavor to another and resetting seemingly gigantic goals on a total whim. It's like the opposite of sunk cost fallacy; the 2iC might set a goal that takes twelve months to achieve, get halfway there, and then abandon it wholesale for seemingly no outside reason.

Because a 2iC can see so many things so broadly, it can be difficult to find confidence in their own choices about what is important. While they're dogged to the point of being offensive when they latch on to something, they can be flippant when they're not.

2iCs *Do* Have Some Outsized Ego and Drive

This ties heavily into the other character traits, but once you point a 2iC in a direction, they tend to become incredibly competitive. Nathan has said many times that he wants to be at the top of the leaderboard... but he doesn't really care *which* leaderboard.

Without that direction, they still have all the energy within them to be highly competitive, but they'll typically direct that inward to self-improvement or outward to their perception of what is good (which probably feeds their intense imposter syndrome and curiosity).

CHAPTER 8

WHY ISN'T BEING SECOND KNOWN AND CELEBRATED?

THE WORD "SECOND" is typically a measure of relative position in a tangible or intangible hierarchy. Without a first, the traditional concept of being second would be rendered meaningless. In this understanding, a "second position" has fallen short of the assumed attempt to occupy the first role. Think of a race. Everyone enters to try to be first, but it is a zero-sum game. By certain rules, someone occupies first, and this means that everyone else does not. And it is unusual for someone to ultimately try to occupy the second position.

The transference of this logic to the most functional domains of life is distorted and unrealistic at best, stigmatizing and damaging at worst.

In reality, being a Second has virtually nothing to do with coming in second place. The distinctions are not restrictive. Instead, these distinctions are *descriptive*—they describe a complementary set of leadership skills needed to fill out a total suite of required leadership needs.

Seconds are *willing to serve*. Their ambition is tied to their position description, not to their position ranking. A Second is kicked into creative gear by the upstream and external force of a cause, one that is often embodied by whoever is in the First in Command role. The First in Command can be a sufficient cause that kicks a Second into action. In no way does this diminish the creative potential of a Second—this interdependence is just the ideal condition for a Second's creative potential.

But language and culture can't be separated, and in our Western culture we've provided no language for this dynamic. Without language we can't even tell a story. Without stories, we struggle to understand people and nuances and all we're left with are simplistic structures like first place and second place.

One of the main distinctions between what has come to be known as "Eastern" and "Western" cultures is that of collectivism vs. individualism. While there is undoubtedly some nuance across countries and cultures, and it is dangerous to ask broad sociological distinctions to bear too much weight, this distinction does shed light on how societies have viewed and esteemed leaders and crowned heroes across history.

Western culture has tended towards individualism—perhaps increasingly in recent years—and has tended to look towards individuals at tops of hierarchies. "Leadership" has often been collocated within individual leaders; a "leader" is imbued with the idea that a person should possess *all* aspects of leadership. While a "leadership team" is certainly a common concept in the West, it contains certain paradoxes. If a leader is supposed to have the full gamut of leadership qualities, then what does it mean to have a team of leaders? The logical implication is that you'll have redundant types of leaders, only differentiated in *what* they oversee, not *how* they oversee. And no matter how valuable a Second might be, they traditionally have not been valued as a leader in the West the way a top individual leader is.

The combination of individualism and independence as Western values can blind people to the idea that leadership is distributed across people by function and not just within a monolithic group of leaders.

In statistics, we often talk of tests that look at differences *between* vs. *within* groups. Using this idea, we can say that "leaders" are all lumped *within* one group based on one kind of leadership. In that framework, Seconds would naturally have different average scores on different leadership attributes. If you only value leadership aspects as to those typically associated with First in Commands or Artisans, Seconds will look like inferior leaders. However, if you separate the concept of leadership from ideals of individualism and independence, there is suddenly a wide-open field of leaders that can still exhibit leadership, even it looks a bit (or significantly) different.

Looking for differences outside of lists of narrow leadership attributes permits the open field we need for the task of this book: looking for (and validating) differences *between* different types of leaders before looking for quantitative differences *within* those different types of leaders.

Excerpt from a panel interview with Beth Carr and Mondo Davison. Interview conducted by David and Nathan.

Beth Carr: I do think there's a cultural layer, always, even in grade school. Did you win; did you come in first? Second isn't as remembered. You think of track and field on the Olympics right now—they don't talk about the person who is less than three tenths of a second behind the winner, the winner's the winner. We even say it in entertainment, right? There's the *lead* singer. No one's talking about the drummer. The drummer has to go off and do his own thing and become Ringo.

If you really strip that all back, it's about ego. And to claim being a number two is setting aside, not only that ego, but actually enjoying the new swagger of being the Doer and the Executor and being okay with other people being in the spotlight.

What I loved when Nathan approached me about being on this panel was, yeah, there's so many closeted Seconds. I think this book is going to help bring in a new cultural story that will encourage more people that, actually, Second is sometimes more important than that podium gold spot. And how cool is that? There might be new threads sewn into the fabric of, "It's okay to be the second. It's actually more important to be."

David Hartman: And it seems to play out over and over and over again. What I hear you saying is it's more egalitarian, right? It's not about being on a podium. It's like, "What do we need to do to get stuff done? What people do we need in our org chart to be able to move things forward?" But it's hard to break that. Instantly people shift into sitting on the pedestal, like, "Who's up highest?"

Mondo Davison: I'll just say real quick that I just think the story hasn't been told. As I'm hearing this, I'm thinking a lot about the *Hidden Figures* story, the Black women from NASA, right? Until the story is told, it's not valued. The work was valued to somebody at that point, but not to the broader audience. As soon as the story becomes a mainstream story, how that number one and number two work together, I think it'll be celebrated a lot more.

Why We Hear about the Role and Not the Identity

At its core, language is the method of moving thoughts and feelings from inside your head to outside of it. Communication is when we use language together, and communicating with each other can be difficult even in the best of times. Language differences can make it exponentially more difficult—and if you think speaking different languages makes communication hard, it becomes nearly impossible when language changes over time.

Forsooth, amirite?!

Language doesn't just change by the addition of words to our dictionaries. We also change the meaning of words that already have definitions. The word "enable" is Nathan's current favorite example of adjusting the meaning of a word that already exists. It's a really wholesome and straightforward word with a clear opposite: enable/disable. Like, "make it work" and "make it not work", right?

But here's the description of "enable" from Merriam Webster in 2022:

Enable has a number of senses, most of which are some variant on allowing someone (or something, such as enabling cookies on a computer) to do something.

In the past several decades, enable has also started to take on a new associated sense in the field of addiction studies, where enabling is viewed as giving misguided support to a person with some substance-abuse issue. A person who facilitates the self-destructive behavior of another is referred to as an enabler.

Well... that's quite confusing.

(Aside: where does that leave "disable"?)

The "enable" issue makes you *think* you're speaking the same language, but you're *not*.

Similarly, we discussed earlier that one of the issues making it difficult to talk about Seconds is that, at least in more Western cultures, we equate "being Second" to "coming in second place" or "Silver Medalist." Effectively, we collectively think that "Second" is "lesser."

We here in this book now know that "Second" being "lesser" when speaking in a hierarchical sense could not be further from the truth. But we're all playing against a stacked deck, so to speak.

Nathan

Did you know that, speaking in math terms, one is actually closer to zero than two? Two is actually, literally "greater than" one. Actually, one is only "bigger" than two when they're both negative. Thinking of 2 as "less than" one is literally negative thinking. Yeah, I'm a nerd. What.

We've noticed another funny language thing along this journey, and it's been a helpful anchor even as we add needed nuance. It is that roles exist, like jackets to be worn.

They will be filled no matter what, and some people are naturally suited to them.

That probably feels like it makes perfect sense as you read it and/or hear it, but it really has been an effort to draw those two concepts apart. Enough that it feels important to point it out as an issue.

We speak with a lot of people who use or are familiar with various business operating systems (which are great!)—but it has meant that words like "Visionary" have started being equated with roles, in the vernacular of those systems.

Why is that an issue?

Because words like "Visionary" are *also* used to describe natural human traits.

When said this way, it effectively conflates the trait and role. That would be like stitching "Perfect Pitch" on a jacket and considering it an indication of a trait.

A jacket is something you can take off and give to someone else, but perfect pitch is personal. Handing someone a jacket that has "perfect pitch" sewn on it does not confer that trait to the next person to put the jacket on. Similarly, you can call a role "The Visionary," but being in the role of the Visionary is something you can take off and give to someone else. *Being visionary* is a personal trait that cannot be passed along.

That probably got some people up in arms, so do us a favor and swap the name of the Visionary role to "Master of the Universe" instead. Same position, pay, whatever—just change the title. See how it rolls around in your head. Does that feel different? If it does, why? Now try "Queen" instead. Same effect?

That mental exercise helped us realize that the name of the role kept changing our expectations of the traits of who was filling the role, even though the role itself did not change.

The same goes for "Integrator." The book *Traction* by Gino Wickman explains the role of the Integrator in the EOS system by calling out some of the work that the role is expected to do, as well as calling out the natural traits that a person should have if they're a good fit for that role. But "Integrator" is still just the name of a specific role in a specific system, and you can be handed the Integrator role as easily as you're handed a jacket. Wearing the jacket—a.k.a., being in the role—does not change who you are as a person. Similarly, who you are as a person does not change the expectations of the role.

We've seen plenty of examples of companies that "installed" the system, as they say, and renamed whoever was sort of doing project management with that new title—then months later decide that they weren't actually the "right" person, they didn't do the stuff like the book talked about, or basically, they weren't a "natural." That makes perfect sense *if* the role and the person are totally separate. Without a clear understanding that there's a *role* and, separately, a *person*, some weird things start happening.

For one, it leads to people identifying and communicating their whole identity, and their value, by something that can be taken away and given to someone else as easily as a jacket.

It also gets really convoluted, really fast. Lack of clear definition leads to a lot of confusion, poor communication, and poor decision making. Once you've conflated this thing and stuffed it all into too few words, you end up slicing it all so thin trying to understand what each other are saying that nobody can bear talking about it anymore.

That's why you hear about the role and not the person: we *literally* haven't had a word to put the idea of the person into, and the most obvious word (Seconds) has a dumb connotation because of our culture. We should probably call it a mubchubber or something... except not that because that's a stupid word. ASKDFHAGSOY. Someday, maybe we'll pick some words from Old Latin or something, loosely translated to what we're talking about, and people can call us all *those* words instead of Seconds and 2s and 2iCs. We'll be *Legates* or *Secundo di Emperium*—super cool stuff like that.

Or maybe, someday, thanks to conversations like these, language will shift and being Second won't be such a weird thing anymore.

Here's another excerpt from the interview Nathan did with Kristie Clayton, founder of Female Integrator Mastermind, and experienced EOS Integrator. We feel like this encapsulates what we're trying to say here.

Kristie: So, clarifying question—when you are using the term COO, can you define for me which one you are? What acronym you're using here?

Nathan: Yeah, so I mean it as a Second in Command role. Sort of colloquially with "the Right Hand of the CEO."

Kristie: So, like a Chief Opera*ting* officer?

Nathan: Yes. Not a Head of opera*tions*.

Kristie: Okay. That is one thing for me that I'm seeing a lot of people have a lot of confusion around. When you say COO, they immediately think Chief Operations Officer. And even though it's opera*ting*, they are still calling it opera*tions*. And I'm like, those are two totally different things, people!

Nathan: And the mindset of those two people is not the same.

Kristie: Exactly. Because you have a great operations mind and you may be a COO in that role, does not mean you're an opera*ting* and that you can easily switch in and out. It doesn't work that way.

Nathan: I'm glad you said that. One of the things we're struggling with the mightiest is language. Purely, there is not enough language. So, way too many concepts are being bundled up in way too few words.

Kristie: Yes. Could not agree more.

Nathan: That's part of why we've broken this out. At first, we went about asking, "What does it mean to be an Integrator?"
Then we were like, well, not everyone who is like this is an Integrator, because not everyone runs on the EOS sys-

tem. It's not like you only are that person if you run on EOS. That's a system that finds people to put into that role. So the system just recognized the person.

Kristie: Mm-hmm.

Nathan: So what do you do? Let's assume EOS never goes away, but in an alternate reality where it does, in ten years, all these people who were like, "Well, I was an Integrator and I had value. EOS is gone, but I'm the same person."

Kristie: Mm-hmm.

Nathan: Like, is this how we lose magic in the world?

Kristie: Well, and Nathan, I would even say it's slightly different than what you're explaining too, because EOS where you're at is on it, right? It's everywhere. Everybody knows it. If you are walking around in Minneapolis, you know what EOS is. However, in the south it is still pretty uncommon. People don't know it nearly as well. I'm hearing it more and more—you know, for a long time I used the title Integrator, and I spent so much time explaining what that meant. Eventually we just said, "Ah, give it up."

We need to have an external title that makes sense, right? Because people just didn't understand it. Now what we settled with is that our Visionary is our CEO and I am the President of our company. Because again, that COO role, it's confusing.

Nathan: Yes. That's something we're absolutely trying to establish clarity around.

ROLES VS. IDENTITY (AND ROLES ASKING FOR IDENTITY)

A little back and forth between Nathan and David, extolling the need for the role because of the identity.

Nathan: I find the role of COO to be necessary because of what I hit my head on: I need that second type role to exist because there has to be a place for me. If I'm just on the line, I'm gonna go insane. Because I can see the whole system, but also I don't want to be "First." Like what Jeff was talking about earlier, he didn't wanna be an actor, he needed to lead the whole production—but not to envision or write or sell it.

David: Fantastic. So that mutual need again—it's like we need to have a role to unlock the best of us and to make sense of ourselves. I think there is kind of a formlessness to the identity right now, right? We have movie types of the First in Command, the Visionary, you know? But not Seconds.

You watch the *West Wing* and there's certain leadership styles that are put up front. The Chief of Staff is probably not the hero of the story. My wife is a Chief of Staff, so I can speak to that. She's smarter than me, too. She couldn't be on this call because she's too busy getting things done.

…

I REMEMBER hearing about a concept in grad school that's been a useful analytical tool with broad application for me ever since. One of my professors referred to a "logic of confidence"—which basically referred to the fact that administrators and parents of students could be confident that educators can be trusted to do their assigned work activities with no oversight. The idea is that, when you close a classroom door, we have a logic of confidence that what is happening in the classroom is educative. This means that, by default, those who are exposed to the conditions of a classroom will become educated (in a way that means something definitive, transferable, and somewhat universal).

We see organizations use this same construct of a "logic of confidence" to think about people's performance in certain roles. By default, it is often thought that employees are performing their roles because of the job description attached to the role. The job title and job description inhere in an employee by virtue of accepting a job. The logic of confidence would say, "This is getting done because we have someone in that role." No need to think much more about it.

In essence, an employee is a blank canvas that is shaped and colored by the job title and job description.

However, there are certain roles that are not transposable or interchangeable in terms of those who occupy them. Some roles are malleable enough to accommodate a reasonably malleable person. You can have confidence that some roles can be reasonably accomplished by an array of people. But some roles call for a certain mold of person. The role itself, no matter how clearly defined, cannot mold an individual to its form and function.

Let's use a simple analogy to (kind of) illustrate this point: You could talk about what you need a basketball to do to function as the object used in the sport of basketball. It needs to bounce, be transferable to other players, and be able to be launched into a basketball hoop—and all of these using human hands. This is a "job description" for a basketball.

Now, from this perspective, could an NFL football do the trick? Sure. But you're starting to see the point. We could tighten the job description by adding: has to be round, has to bounce predictably... But with these additions, the role could still go to a dodgeball or a soccer ball.

This is where the analogy breaks down a bit. You could probably add elements to a description for a basketball and come up with something close to what we know as a modern basketball. But some job roles cannot guarantee that the role is being accomplished by simple virtue that they are exhaustively defined. They need a certain type of person, a certain identity—the job description emanates from *within* the employee in a way that the job description is only trying to capture and keep up with.

If you've ever been the kid that tried to play basketball with a soccer ball because it was the only ball you had, you know it is underwhelming. And if you're an organization that has tried to define its way to having a Second, you've likely felt the pain of trying to squeeze a non-Second into a Second mold with external pressure. It just isn't the same.

The fact that Seconds are often understood as a combination of elements in a job description and not as an intrinsic set of gifts and disposition points to a lack of widely perceived value. Occupying a second role is an identity in a certain sense of the word "identity" – there is an aspect of identity that is flat, descriptive: an identity can be a distinction about the contours of a social or professional role. But "identity" can also refer to fact that someone receives a sense of social meaning (a sense of self) and importance within a role or aspect someone possesses. In other words, there's a difference between *having an identity (role, social category, etc.) conferred upon you* and *finding a sense of identity (meaning, significance).*

In general, when you don't hear about an identity (in the sense of a role or social category), it often reveals that there's not shared widespread social value ascribed to it. The less shared social value around a role, the less potential that role has to confer identity (in the meaning-and-significance sense) to the individual who occupies the role.

With this context in mind, it would make sense that not hearing about Second as an identity would be an extension of the outsized historical importance we've placed on those in the First in Command role.

It seems generally true that there has been a conflation of the concept of "leader" and "a singular role and person at the top of an organization imbued with all facets of leadership." The refinement and nuance of research on different types of intelligence, different leadership styles, and different leadership aspects have paved a way to our work in solidifying forms of intelligence, leadership styles, and leadership aspects for a fairly stable recurring archetype: the Second.

The spate of recent leadership research has sparked a frenzy of a proliferation of leadership and intelligence combinations that leave the idea of single, irreducible quality of "leadership" untenable. First in Commands are an important type of leader, but they can hardly stand alone in organizational leadership. The totality of types of leadership and intelligence required to run organizations cannot all inhere in one role or one individual.

It has also allowed us to see value in organizations possessing different types of leaders, and among the most important of those leaders? Seconds. We want to isolate the Second roles that have emerged from recent research and elevate the identity infused in those roles. Seconds need the power that comes from recognizing themselves not just for what they do, but who they are.

Women and the Second Role, Historically Speaking

David

Throughout human history as we understand it, two things in general were happening:

1) Cultures and their historical narratives did not prize or recognize Seconds, even though they understood the necessity of having someone in the role. It was always about the strongest, the hero, the First, in a zero-sum power game. These were typically men and recorded in history as men, whether those men were naturally suited to their roles or not.

And 2) roles that required or called for many attributes of Seconds existed and were necessary in those historical societies, and women were culturally required to do them, especially in domestic arrangements. Again, whether they were naturally suited to the role or not.

Nathan and I both know exceptional women who identify as Seconds *and* those who *DO NOT*, all of whom are incredible performers in their chosen roles—caregiver or CEO or whatever in between.

Given the reality of modern domestic and employment relationships and the broader organizational ability for people to choose roles that fit themselves, or for organizations to choose people that fit available roles, it means that more men *and* women are able to occupy roles that fit them as people.

This example is sort of a microcosm of the entire concept: societally, we've had these roles exist that required certain talents; we treated them as "secondary" or hierarchical rather than egalitarian; and then we pushed an entire gender into that role, totally ignoring the capacity of the individual.

Likely, billions of people have languished in their roles, with women forced to live in the Second role and men forced to live in the First role no matter their personality.

CHAPTER 9

HOW TO BE (A BETTER) SECOND

AS WITH MOST THINGS, developing as a Second (who you are) and developing in your role (what you do right now) are intertwined. Learning how to be a better manager can easily tie in with learning to be a better person overall. But our job isn't really to tell you how to be better in your role. We're here to say that becoming more of who you already are—and more secure in the things you do naturally—will make you better in your role, or at least make you more inclined to find a role where your natural talents and energy shine.

While there aren't many books about developing as the COO or Second in Command, the ones that do exist were written by people with a lot of experience across sizable companies. We feel like pointing towards those in the resources section is the best way to support your professional growth. That's in chapter 11, and we're almost there. But having the nuance of identity that we've discovered through this work has made our own experience of reviewing those books and pulling wisdom out of them that much better. We're now able to spot where "role improvement" books are asking for someone to be better at something that is more likely to be a right person issue than a skill issue. We hope you'll find that same clarity.

However, in hearing the question asked dozens of times and asking the question ourselves, here are some things that more mature Seconds—some 2s and some 2iCs—have said should be areas of focus for self-improvement.

Focus on Your Own Development

Seconds seem to have a natural tendency to shrug off their own personal or professional development as a priority. Instead, they focus on "what needs done" and either think that there will be time to focus on themselves in the future or that it just doesn't matter in comparison to making sure the now things are done now.

There's no kind way to say this—that's dumb. You wouldn't hesitate to upgrade a tool if you knew it was cost-effective and would reduce the workload by 25 percent. You're the same; you'll be way more effective, and the cost is almost always a pittance.

The tendency to kick yourself to the back of the line seems to be two-fold:

- One: Self-improvement is rarely quantifiable. We get that. It's not an excuse, but we get it.
- Two: You're focusing on what needs done now and the organization of now. You're not thinking about the next organization or your next stage of life.

But most likely, there *will* be a next stage of life and a next organization. Also, if you do really well in your current organization, it will probably grow and you'll need new skills anyway.

You need to get used to sharpening yourself (like a tool) to tackle not only what you're doing now, but what you'll *eventually* be doing. Even if it isn't quantifiable today.

Get in *Any* Kind of Peer Group

The (by now) old adage of "if you're the smartest person in the room, you're in the wrong room" has proven helpful time and again. And yes, having people around you that can level you up across the whole range of personal and professional tools is awesome. Some of our colleagues call this "leaning into your utilitarian empathy," how you can get all those professional supports *and* build some relationships at the same time. It's also awesome to not be alone.

That's all well and good, but perhaps the most important aspect of getting into one or more peer groups is the network. Tim Sanders said, "Your network is your net worth," and sure, that's pithy... but seriously. You're going to be head down across ten different areas of the organization, and that does not naturally lend itself to networking outside of your org. But growing your network is building the asset that provides future opportunities for doing cool things and possibly getting paid for those things.

At some point, you'll want to join another group, and you'll need to convey all of this insane and wonderful value that you bring. And as a Second, that still requires a herculean effort. Obviously, we're hoping to help change that, but part of the change we can foster is that we can tell you, *right now*, that your network is one of the most important assets you have, and you need to care for and grow it.

You know what the easiest way to convey your value to a brand-new person is? Having one of the connections you share with that person vouch for you. Person-to-person referrals are still the strongest indicators of trust in the world.

There are more and more peer groups popping up for Second in command type roles, which are attracting people who might identify as Seconds. We'll try to mention a few in the resources section even though groups like that can be a little transient, but know that a bunch of them exist even if that list ages a bit. (Also, you can just email us for the current list of whatever groups we know about right then – we'll make a referral!)

Get a Coach

A coach is not your spouse, not your peer group, and not your boss. Get an outside coach who can help you develop as a person so you're not worried about performing poorly in front of them. Well, not *as* worried. Coaches are meant to help you understand where you are between one and ten, build a workable plan for getting you closer to ten, and keep you accountable for putting that work in.

It's basically what you do for everyone else around you, but when you're inside the jar, it's hard to read the label. You need someone outside the jar who has done the work so you trust their competence enough to follow their plan. (*You* are the jar in this metaphor)

Don't be afraid to swap coaches, either. Not everyone is created equal, and not everyone knows what ten is. There are definitely people out there who say they're an eight of ten, but after a couple sessions you'll realize you already know more than they do, and you don't trust their plan. Don't sweat it—it's probably not malicious, it's just ignorance, and for a lot of people they'll do great. Swap coaches and move on.

And of course, watch for patterns where you're the only constant. If you swap coaches four times because they're all incompetent, the pattern points to you, and you may need to invest in your coach-choosing skills.

Pick a Depth of Focus

Needing or wanting to be the "Expert Generalist" who understands every core area of the thing means you'll be inclined, when going into a new role or studying a new thing, to dig into the systems that underpin the whole machine *and* to understand the vision of the mountaintop.

For the Second in Command role in business orgs, that means having a decent grasp of Sales, Marketing, Operations, Finance, Legal, Admin, IT, Hiring, Planning, Managing, and Partnering.

As Seconds mature (both 2s and 2iCs), they realize that code-switching between this top level and the granular level is either too hard or sort of a waste of time. It's nice to know how the machine works, but it's not actually that important for leading a team that works together well. At some point, it will be best to choose to either dig into the details and know that you'll specialize there with your teams, or to go broader in your perspective and cut your own curiosity off at the knees when it tries to get granular.

Template Things

There seems to be a progression you go through as a Second regarding templates and systems. As Seconds, we inherently understand that you can't use something one-for-one forever. It gets you in trouble in sales emails, it gets you in trouble at scale, and it gets you in trouble in relationships. So your gut reaction might be to just start building the system or process you need. Between the two of us, we've built hundreds of hacked together spreadsheets and we've seen hundreds more. Flowcharts, diagrams, note-taking systems, whatever. It's easy to just craft what you need from scratch.

Learn to resist this urge.

If you can hack something together in a few minutes—sure, great. Most likely though, someone else has already put something together that will solve the issue and might even contain some new ideas that jump you forward. Some Seconds (especially 2iCs) will be frustrated by this idea, since nothing out there can be *exactly* what *you* need, but that's where templates come in.

A template can be as simple as step one, step two, step three, with some bullet points for customization. As a Second, you probably understand what we're getting at here. You *will* need to customize, but you certainly don't need to start from scratch. Also, you're not an imposter if you rip off and duplicate; just don't forget that customization.

Be a Raving Fan

As a Second, you have as much ability as anyone to spot everything that's going wrong. How to improve things, how the system is broken, whatever. It won't take long to understand that *everything* is this way—there is no promised land of everything working perfectly smoothly all the time forever, at least not in this life.

That means you should be part of things—or choose some things—to be a raving fan of. If your natural inclination is to be willing to serve, be a great follower, and teach others how to follow well, then find something you can say "I love it" about. Find things to imbed yourself in that you're a raving fan of.

That doesn't mean "if you find something you love you won't work a day." We don't believe in that. Work is hard, and there's nothing wrong with that. We're saying be a raving fan of the stuff you're part of. Your group, your hobbies, your leaders, your team, whatever. Find some stuff to be a raving fan of.

Leave

If you have a job where you're being stretched thin and no one appreciates that, start by having a discussion about feeling that way. It's really unlikely that *anyone* understands exactly how much you're doing, so try not to dumpster them assuming they're doing it on purpose.

It seems reasonable that if we're delegating our futures up to our leadership teams all day to expect to be respected in return. For reasons that are most often ignorance and not malicious at all, they don't know to do anything different than what's happening. Which makes sense—a lot of people are already doing the best they can, including you, right? Your life isn't their life, and your plan probably isn't their plan. And that's fine.

But if you can't get on the same page, don't wallow there feeling unrecognized and disrespected. If you've had the conversations, been generous while standing up for yourself, and recognized your own value—and still no one cares? Leave.

If you can't be a raving fan, leave.

Don't let yourself get trapped feeling like the whole thing will fall apart if you leave.

Find something else.

Leave.

Maybe it *will* fall apart, which would (probably) suck, but you can always go join another thing that's similar and probably better for you. And maybe the organization you left will learn a valuable lesson in the process. (But don't leave to teach them a lesson; that usually doesn't work.)

Leaving can be terrifying for a ton of reasons, but (with some exceptions) it's important to remember that it's an option.

If you *do* have to leave, try to leave as well as possible. "Don't burn bridges," as Nathan's wife often says.

Seasons and Fit

You may have a season with an organization. It's possible to do an excellent job and have the organization simply grow past your current abilities.

You may be the right person to take the COO seat, you may naturally understand the role—but you may also tap out at a certain size company or a certain level of complexity in any organization.

It's not just about finding your seat on the bus; it's also about finding the right bus.

If this happens and you can keep perspective, it should

be bittersweet. Saying goodbye is hard most of the time, but no longer being the right person is likely because you *were* the right person for a while and did a great job while you were there.

For 2iCs: Grow Your People Skills

When asked whether it's important to develop relationships, most 2iCs will answer, "Of course, because (XYZ reason)."

Whereas most 2s will answer, "Of course."

When talking about growing their skills, almost every 2iC says they need growth in "interpersonal skills." It's almost like skills around people were hedged out to make room for their other unique traits.

Growing your people skills doesn't need to mean pushing against who you are, but it does mean using your unique skills to build those relationships. A tactic to connect with people better that Nathan picked up from a coach is "listening to the core." Instead of creating metaphor and analogy using whatever pops into his head, he listens to the person to understand constructs they already know, then attempts to communicate in their known language. For example, if someone likes golf and you don't know anything about golf, but you make the attempt to use golf stuff for your analogy anyway. Most speakers of foreign languages will tell you it's endearing that you're even making the attempt, and sometimes it's actually helpful to improve communication because they'll explain it for you and you can adjust with them to find nuances. Either way, you're building the relationship between you.

Listening to the core is just a single, small tactic within this area, but it seems to be something to specifically focus on for 2iCs.

Pick a Message, Repeat the Message

If people don't really pick up on what you're trying to say until you repeat it seven times (or seventy times), you really only have to choose a few things that you're going to say a lot. This feels like a lesson for all Seconds, but especially 2iCs since we see so many things that it's easy for us to have something to say about everything.

Pick your North Stars and stick with them. You know, things like "know your own value," "the role is not the identity," and "competence is not the same as energy."

Relationships between 2s, 2iCs, and First in Commands

In talking about 2s and 2iCs and the First in Command role, we've created what we feel is an obvious gap that needs filled—the 1iC, which we defined and talked about a little bit earlier.

If Seconds are collectively "naturally suited" to sit as Second in Command or Right Hand, the 1iC is that "natural" type person who is the Crazy Entrepreneur, the vision caster, the big idea person, or the one crazy dancing person. You get it—we don't need to wax poetic about this one. There's been plenty of ink spilled already explaining this person and the roles they end up in.

As usual for this book, we're focused on talking about

the person, not the role. So when we say 1iC, that's what we mean. We'll stick with 1iC as the person and First in Command for the role.

When the 1iC type is working day-to-day, they're often in one of two places—either in the clouds or the weeds.

On a positive side, when 1iCs are on the mountaintop, it's easy for Seconds of either type to feel confident "delegating up," as the 1iC's ability to see the future brings a lot of comfort. When the 1iC is down in the weeds, they're usually working side by side specifically with 2s, which can bring a sense of togetherness for both. (Even if the 1iC being in the weeds makes the 2iC pretty nervous or downright annoyed.)

On the negative side, when the 1iC jumps to the mountaintop, they expect 2s to follow. When 2s don't go to the mountaintop with them, it leaves the 1iC feeling alone and frustrated, wondering why their Right Hand suddenly feels cut off. 2s can feel frustrated that the 1iC isn't making any sense even as the 1iC feels like the 2s can't keep up with them. It can go from feeling like a peer relationship to extreme frustration, with the 1iC asking, "How do you not get it?"

Also, when a 1iC gets into the weeds without warning, they can bring a sense of things being done wrong, at a pedantic level of detail. 2s who have been operating and managing everything at their own level without support from leadership other than general direction, can feel like the 1iC is just dropping in and messing everything up. They might want to scream, "Get out of my room!" at the 1iC.

This negative scenario happens a lot when 1iCs and 2s are working without a 2iC to act as a bridge.

1iCs and 2s can work just fine for a while—it's not necessarily devastating. But 1iCs and 2s without a 2iC will likely work under a constant, *unnecessary* tension of unrealized expectations.

2s may have a tough time looking beyond the hierarchy they choose for permission to do what they feel is necessary. "Going around" their manager/boss/authority to the next level, or leaving the organization or team altogether, can be a nearly impossible ask of a 2.

1iC/2iC pairings are often incredibly healthy for the 2iC because of the tendency of the 2iC to cast themselves about restlessly. The almost endless energy that 1iCs seem to have for not just picturing the future, but also for being willing to convince anyone and everyone how important it is that it comes into being, keeps a 2iC motivated and focused. It's almost like the 1iC's natural tendency to generate ideas pairs perfectly with the extra attention the 2iC has, as the 2iC has to spend all that energy swatting away those extra ideas and keeping the team focused.

Negatively, 1iCs and 2iCs tend to speak different languages. 1iCs are often not clear on the value and process of a 2iC. Consequently, 1iCs think their vision should be manifested with little delay or organizational strain. A 1iC can so clearly see the mountaintop of what their vision will look like when completed. But they don't see what a "sherpa" 2iC sees: the reality of the terrain that comes between this point and the mountaintop ahead. And if a 1iC cannot see the realities of the terrain, they are unable to prepare to be able to tackle the terrain. They can become impatient and leave a 2iC in a frustrating position of not being able to feel competent because a 1iC hasn't counted the cost of their vision.

Finally, all Seconds will struggle with a 1iC who is addicted to vision that feels new and exciting to them. Given the time lag between casting and fulfilling vision, 1iCs of a certain stripe can become restless and uninspired by the vision that the Seconds are presently trying to fulfill. Here again, we bump up against all Seconds' need for feeling competent and being followers. Their sense of competence is inextricably tied to the vision of whoever is in the First in Command role in the group they're part of. The First in Command, no matter what kind of person it is, galvanizes and energizes Seconds with purpose and interest to perform in their own roles. When the First in Command is a 1iC with a tendency to change the target all the time, a Second's ability to feel competent is extended into the future as they are left to reboot their strategy and plans or to adjust and explain to their teams. It can create a strong sense of helplessness and incompetence.

When 1iCs and 2iCs are paired together, the 1iC doesn't have the ability to change as often as they want. That means that 2s don't have to spend as much of their energy convincing their teams to change course, and can instead focus on developing and coaching. Both the 2iC and 2s get to feel a sense of competence and progression in this case, and in the end, everyone involved *does* move tangibly closer to the mountaintop.

Nathan

A setup that's been fascinating for me to navigate is my current job. I'm the Second in Command, which is great; I'm solidly in my spot as a 2iC. That being said, the person who I serve as my First in Command is *also* a 2iC by identity. Hilariously to me, there's *another* 2iC filling a role as a department head, and a natural 1iC who is in the head of sales role. Thank the Lord in heaven, we have several 2s serving throughout the rest of the team.

I think it's fairly likely that without this book, the three of us natural 2iC types would have plotted the demises of each other within the first few days, or our headbutting would have just killed us off. However, as I've been studying this identity in us, I've been able to start speaking to each of us for who we are. I know when my First in Command will zig zag before he does most of the time—it actually annoyed him at first (and occasionally still does, ha!).

I'm also not the smartest person in the room, not even close—both of the other 2iCs around me are definitely smarter and more experienced than I am. But I am very aware of our natural strengths and energy and able to speak to and navigate those things, or occasionally predict and avoid them entirely. For instance, I've been able to fill in gaps in our thinking and request that we deploy our on-staff 1iC to situations where we need a little more of that energy.

My First in Command and I *do* have a way harder time staying on the same page, as we're both trying to sort of "beautiful mind" our way to solutions. But you can't have two plans to march out. That has been a challenge and probably will continue to be that way.

I actually love my job right now, and the education I'm getting about both the roles and the identities has been fascinating! But it definitely goes to show that 1iCs aren't always in the First in Command role, 2iCs aren't always in the Second in Command role, and so on.

All told, 1iC/2iC/2 pairings tend to average out as the most healthy for everyone, which helps explain why our human built hierarchies seem to end up with those roles being available so consistently.

COMMON STRUGGLES OF SECONDS (BOTH OF THEM)

Personality assessments or conversations about identity often focus on the positive aspects of who you are and what you have to bring to the world. Which is great! But what about the low branches that you're likely to smack your head on?

We've discussed some of the back and forth tendencies and traits of 2s and 2iCs and how you're awesome, so here's what we found as common issues for you as well.

Seconds and Taking Feedback

For all Seconds, but especially for young 2iCs early in your career or personal development: you may take feedback very personally. You're working so hard that *any* feedback feels like being told you're not good enough. That's not what it actually is, but it's easy to feel that way.

Anyone who has said they have this skill completely figured out is lying. (Including us.)

Seconds, Imposter Syndrome, and Valuing Yourself

Most of the traits of Seconds (both 2s and 2iCs) lead to them feeling like imposters in almost every position they're in. It seems like everyone in the world feels like this at some level, which is a topic for another day, but Seconds tend to struggle longer and more intensely with this across every area of their lives.

On one hand, it's not uncommon to see Seconds in higher level leadership positions like the C-Suite, Director, or Manager, and yet, even while they hold that position and other people think the Second is incredible in their role, the Second is waiting to be found out as a fraud.

We have a phrase for this. We call it, "knowing what ten is." A generalist skillset, combined with curiosity and interest in people, means Seconds are more aware of the full breadth of a skill. They tend to uncover what mastery looks like in skills they take interest in, and then compare themselves against mastery. In other words, on a scale of ten, they know what one is and what ten is, as well as the distance between the two, and they rate themselves between those points.

If a Second were to become interested in basketball, they'd be curious enough to study Jordan, Bird, and LeBron to help themselves understand what "good" really is—what ten is. They'd also study types of offense and defense, tactics, the mind of the game, agility and ball handling drills, and they'd put actual reps in for muscle memory. Then, after putting in work and gaining knowledge, they'd be nervous about their own skill level because they're keenly aware of how far they still are from what a ten really is.

This is actually a double whammy; while the Second is saying "I'm not that great at this" because they're comparing themselves to the people who have gotten as close to ten as possible, their hesitation actually comes off as arrogance to people around them. People around the Second see them they way they actually come off—as above average, or to the right of the bell-curve in both performance and awareness. So the Second's attempts at humility, appropriately founded on their knowledge of what ten is, ends up making them seem like a jerk.

Seconds and Being Disappointed in Others (Because They Know What Ten Is)

While Seconds struggle with their own imposter syndrome because of their broader knowledge of "what ten is", they'll forget that other people don't know what the Second knows. At the same time the Second perceives themselves as almost average at some skill, perhaps a four out of ten on the competence scale, people around the Second will rate themselves as seven out of ten.

This will range from annoying to infuriating for the Second, as the scale is different but the language is the same. People around the Second will say of themselves, "I'm better than average," while the Second perceives those same people as substandard at best.

This can put the Second into another weird position of feeling crazy—as if they're the odd one out, again surrounded by people who know something that they don't know, which plays into that imposter fear.

Most of the times we've seen this, the Second is actually "correct." Their scale of ten is closer to reality than the people around them. Sadly, that's of little comfort, as being correct isn't that helpful in a group—unless you also have the people skills to navigate explaining it and getting people bought in, as well as the self-awareness to know whether you should even make the attempt.

2s and Taking on *Way Too Much*

2s almost always struggle to say "no" of their own volition. This is easier if it's part of taking care of their team—for example, being in a Project Manager role and saying no to an overly demanding client will be easier than saying no to a team member when they ask you to cover their shift.

When 2s say yes to too many things, they tend to have a plate full of wildly different work to do. This kicks off a negative cycle, starting with losing the ability to context switch like they're used to.

That leads to other things like constraints in their curiosity, losing perception of their own value, and actual performance reduction.

2iCs and People Becoming Barriers (to Put It Nicely)

To a 2iC, people around them are to be initially and continually assessed. These assessments are often on a different continuum than how most people assess others. Once a 2iC has a vision of what success looks like and devises a plan for success, it becomes clear what resources are needed to work the plan. People in the organization are often required to successfully work that plan to maintain the 2iCs belief in their competence.

To a 2iC, a person in the organization who either cannot see the value of the plan or who seems unable or unwilling to follow the plan can become an object of derision.

A 2iC is not always initially wired with a bent towards coaching people and developing them to be able to help effect change. A 2iC can become frustrated and begin to see people either as barriers to change (at best) and complete wastes of space (at worst).

2s and Self-Aligning to Serve (While Your Peers Try to See You as Equal)

A 2, when paired up with a 1iC or 2iC in a relationship where they should be peers, will probably start out aligned that way, and then over time re-align themselves as a follower. In reality, it goes back to the 2's natural strengths of follow-ership and being more in control of their own ego than others—but it's typically not perceived that way.

This can cause some interesting dynamics if you pair a 2 and a 2iC together as partners, for example, in a business or as significant others. The 2 will (likely unconsciously) begin to look to their partner as their leader, waiting on the plan and then acting it out, rather than contributing to the plan as a peer. This will require more energy and drive from their partner. In a 2/2iC pairing, a 2iC might get very frustrated with their partner, as they start to perceive themselves as "dragging" the 2 to get anything moved forward.

2iCs and Feeling Lonely (When Seeing What Others Don't)

As we depicted in the "when do you see" graphic, there are areas of overlap and isolation across First in Commands, 2iCs, and 2s. One of the areas of isolation for a 2iC is their ability to see forward into processes, implications, and ultimate consequences.

A 2iC may see that one input will have downstream impact on different outputs and outcomes. A First in Command might be unable to see it, and a 2 may only see the portion of a process that they personally oversee.

Seeing all of the interconnections is the gift and the curse of the 2iC. A First in Command may vacillate between seeing that gift as vital to success or as the curse spoiling the vision. 2iCs can feel lonely in this vacillation. 2iCs feel lonely (and maybe like they're crazy) by seeing and reacting to things and formulating responses that seem unwarranted or nonsensical by a First in Command or a 2.

A 2 may see the implications to a certain extent, but they may be able to ease the psychological toll of the organization not changing course by diving into smaller portions of the process. A 2iC may be left holding the bag, seeing implications and living in a private hell that they often are correct in knowing will be public in the not-too-distant future.

Seconds and Being in Roles They're Not Built For

Having a natural tendency to raise your hand for whatever role the team needs means that Seconds are likely to have a lot of opportunities for roles that will destroy their energy, and occasionally they'll find they lack the competence as well.

It's important that Seconds look after their own energy and to the other pieces of their personality for what they find fulfilling, rather than jumping in wherever they're "needed" the most right then.

For a tough example, being incredible people leaders and broadly competent means there will be pressure to either start your own group or company or be promoted to the First in Command role.

We're not saying there aren't exceptions. There are likely many Seconds out there who fill the First in Command role, and the team, the org, and the world, are better for it.

We do think it tends to be a losing proposition. This is a "just because you can, doesn't mean you should" situation. We believe the likelihood that Seconds will start their own thing, create a job for themselves with a few clients, and end up feeling lonely overall is frustratingly high.

The same is true for a lot of other roles that people might ask them to do. It's great to be what's needed, but in the end, the Second ends up drained, having taken on more than anyone understood, and having stunted their own deeper skill development during that time.

2s and Being Put into the Second in Command Role

In the same way that the First in Command role is likely to be a poor-fitting jacket for all Seconds, being a 2 and being in the Second in Command role is almost guaranteed to fit weird... though, probably not initially.

As a 2, getting assigned to this Second in Command seat probably won't happen at all if you have an experienced leader who knows what the org needs *and*, more importantly, is paying attention to what you need. If you have a less experienced leader who doesn't know what a 2iC relationship feels like, they're likely to promote their Right Hand, which is probably you, as you've already gained the trust of the team and have been great at whatever you've done.

This is a similar situation to when the great salesperson gets promoted to sales manager. We argue that those roles are not linear in progression at all, but are actually two entirely different skillsets. The Second in Command position may be something you want (or not), but typically the position demands behavior that doesn't match how your natural instincts want you to behave.

We've laid out a bunch of them already, but 2s and 2iCs differ on specific parts of their personalities. Some of that is ego, their outsized need to make the plan, higher risk tolerance, and a radical ability to say no. This typically makes a great Yin and Yang for the First in Command/Second in Command style of leadership, as 2iCs will be at their best while corralling the first in command and fighting to stay on the same page.

It's not about being capable—2s are just typically not interested, or don't have the energy, to go toe-to-toe with their leaders all the time in that way. As we say often, it's not about competence, it's about energy.

2iCs and Not Being Trusted to and/or Able to Make Improvements

This challenge is pretty much a death sentence to a 2iC. While a 2 might be able to rally and fall in line, leaning into their followership, a 2iC withers when they are unable to actuate changes they see are needed.

Whether this stems from a lack of trust from their First in Command, a lack of authority invested in the Second in Command position, or just being structurally stuck for any reason, you will see the energy drain from a 2iC in this scenario. They may become irritable, disillusioned, judgmental, and/or depressed.

An inability to make changes rubs against the 2iC's biggest identity need—to feel competent.

COMMON ROLES SECONDS END UP IN

We've talked a lot about natural tendencies and recognizing yourself that way—let's spend some time talking about where those things might have gotten you. This might also be your launching off point. It's possible that a friend of yours read this section, realized they knew someone in one of these roles, and then handed the book to you to see if you were "the thing." If so, welcome!

If you've ever had someone ask what job you could do and your answer was, "Well, anything really!" and you didn't mean, "Please give me *any* job, I'm desperate", but you *actually* meant, "It seems like I can do anything and have worked in every potential role and done pretty well," then we're on track.

Seconds might end up in a huge variety of roles and can become above average in almost all of them with surprising speed.

Because of their willingness to do whatever is needed, Seconds will flow to whatever seems to be the most needed at the time. No matter what role they end up in, their natural curiosity means they tend to already know a lot about whatever they're getting into, or they learn the new parts very quickly.

People around Seconds tend to see them as having twenty hands—the reliable go-to whenever "something" needs done and it doesn't clearly require a specialist.

Even when something *does* require a specialist, Seconds tend to be so reliable and flexible that those things hit their desk first anyway. Seconds are usually being fed a constant stream of new things to at least try, and again, they are likely to find above-average competence fairly quickly, which perpetuates the cycle.

As a combination of these factors and their natural curiosity, Seconds tend to become excellent generalists, highly capable of a strikingly wide array of work.

With all of that being said, there are a few roles that Seconds tend to land in over and over again—and spend a long time there once they do.

COO/Integrator/Chief of Staff/President

These are probably the most common roles that initial readers of this book will hold. These roles seem to have become a sort of home base for all Seconds, which has been incredibly helpful and has created a lot of confusion and frustration at the same time. We don't need to wax any more poetic here about it than we already have all over the place in this book. Just know that if you're in this kind of role and you've picked up this book, it's highly likely that you're in good company.

The Right Hand

One of the sweet spots for Seconds seems to be working as someone's Right Hand. All the traits of a Second's personality mean that it's almost impossible to have a more competent and frankly, loyal, Right Hand than us.

Executive Assistant is often an interchangeable term with the Right Hand, and if anyone thinks this job is easy or a "low skill" position, they've never seen it done well. These positions are often doing half of the role of a COO or Chief of Staff and almost singlehandedly the reason that the rest of the organization is staying on track.

Manager

Seconds tend to do best when there is someone to support, rather than some*thing*, which means their ability to become a People Manager is extraordinary. We believe that this is a specialized skill completely on its own, even though it's not typically treated that way in our Western culture.

Account and Project Manager

"Second" doesn't encapsulate 100 percent of the traits you might have as a person, and we've seen that Account Managers and Project Managers both tend to be great landing spots for Seconds. Some Seconds may have a heavier bent to organization and structure and fit better in project manager roles, whereas other Seconds may be more empathetic or relationship-driven and fit better into Account Manager roles. Either way, these roles ask for the skillsets of Seconds all day long.

Frustrated Artisan

Seconds are likely to get frustrated if they ever decide to focus down an artisanal pathway that is not centered around serving people somehow, and they're likely to end up in a position of people management, seemingly by accident, over and over and over again.

A Second's natural tendencies make it very difficult to focus on a niche skillset—and the micro details of that skillset—long enough to develop ten-of-ten mastery in that thing in the same way that artisans can. If you're in an artisanal position and you've been slamming your head against it for years while constantly getting distracted (and pretty good at) other pursuits, you might be a Second trapped in a too-narrow path.

Other Common Roles:
- First in Command
- Integrator, Team or Division Leader or Manager (Head of Sales, Head of Finance, etc), with a weird penchant for General Management
- Team Lead or Department Manager

- Executive Assistant
- Teacher
- Community Support
- Specialist roles with no traditional training

COMMON ISSUES IN ROLES AND EXPECTATIONS

Seconds might find themselves in all kinds of roles, but there are a few issues with those roles that seem to pop up again and again.

Second in Command Is Not a Good "First in Training" Role

Imagine having a drive that doesn't focus on what is accomplished but how it is accomplished. Imagine being unable to stomach inefficiency, bottlenecks, redundancies, unclear roles, and poor communication. And finally, imagine someone who has the drive to push to the near apex of an organization or business unit...

But.

They typically have no desire to be at the actual apex.

If this sounds familiar, you just might be a 2iC.

And if you're a 2iC, you might be in an organizational structure that values what you do but does not ascribe it worthy of an ultimate destination. You might be looked at in your role with sympathy after holding it for a few years because it is assumed that you are "stuck." And what's worse, you may have bought that assessment.

If what we are proposing is correct (and our research gives us strong conviction that it is), First in Command and Second in Command roles not only perform different work but tend to call for people who identify as different types of people. It is a frequent tactic of capitalistic economies to manufacture personal discontent to keep us striving for (and buying!) more. 2iCs are also frequently told that to fulfill their potential they should strive to become a First in Command. Don't buy it.

A 2iC is a leader-follower. Put in a First in Command role, most 2iCs will become an overbearing technician and will suffocate for vision and inspiration. By the same token, if a natural First in Command is in a Second in Command role as a waiting room to the First in Command role, processual innovation and systematic advances will suffer. People who are natural fits for the Second in Command role will chafe at the expectations once they're placed into the First in Command role, and people who are natural fits for the First in Command role won't wait around for the training and transition to happen.

Paradoxes are notoriously difficult for humans to understand. And 2iCs are a paradox. They lead best by following. We get it—it defies simplistic takes on hierarchy and org structure. A 2iC will muscle their way to nearly the front of the line through profound discontent with poorly performing processes and systems, but that's where they want to hold sway. Don't be confused; you'll see most 2iCs in First in Command roles shrink away from doing the big cultural work that the community expects and hopes for from them and try to find a way to pretend their role is to get into the granular details of performance metrics and system refinement.

A First in Command and Second in Command are a symbiotic set, not a First in Command and someone being groomed to be a First in Command.

Are We Saying Seconds Can't Be "First in Command"?

Nope.

We're not saying that Seconds *can't* be anything. We're saying that, based on the research we've done and conversations we've had, very few Seconds will find something that continuously provides them the energy and fulfillment needed to sustain the incredible pressure and expectations that whoever is in the First in Command role is subject to.

Again, competence does not equal energy, *does not equal fulfillment*.

And to be fair, we're also saying that it's unlikely your natural traits fit well with the cultural expectations of a "good" top of the pyramid leader for our Western culture.

But there are almost always exceptions. Some people who demonstrate that exception are quoted in this book already. Kristie Clayton of FIM is an excellent First in Command for her organization and gets to spend her time doing things that are fulfilling and energizing for her, and Jamie Munoz has built an incredible team as the First in Command of Catalyst Integrators (and loves it).

Promoting Artisans to Second Roles

"Three professors—Alan Benson of the University of Minnesota, Danielle Li of MIT, and Kelly Shue of Yale—analyzed the performance of 53,035 sales employees at 214 American companies from 2005 to 2011. During that time, 1,531 of those sales reps were promoted to become sales managers. The data show that the best sale people were more likely to be a) promoted and b) perform poorly as managers. The Peter Principle is real.

The sales reps in the study, to quote one successful sales manager, were 'promoted not to the level of their incompetence, but OUT of their area of competence.'

...it strikes me that the new research carries a number of important implications. Let me suggest a few:

- *Being an Incredible individual contributor needs to carry more prestige.*
- *You may want to avoid getting promoted.*
- *If a top-selling colleague from your team just became your new boss, it might be time to move on."*

—Rodd Wagner, Forbes Magazine

One issue that has come up several times in our research is a distinction significant enough to warrant a mention and a very preliminary exploration. We ran across a highly skilled and inquisitive subset of people we've come to call Artisans.

From what we can tell, compared to Seconds, Artisans are people who:

1. go deeper in their knowledge or a particular topic,
2. enjoy detail and perfection of a craft, and

3. want to keep their hands in the minutiae of the execution of a process.

By comparison, Seconds will often learn enough about necessary bodies of knowledge to reach an above-average level of competence, but that knowledge is always meant to be instrumental. It is used in the service of a larger process or set of processes. Seconds are more interested in overseeing processes and/or people than fully executing every aspect of the work itself. Basically, Seconds are practically tailor-made to fill managerial roles.

This problem—promoting Artisans to roles that Seconds are suited for—occurs a lot as excellence in one area gets erroneously projected to a different skillset. For instance, the graphic designer who is absolutely amazing at her craft is promoted to a Creative Director role. The problem is, graphic design and overseeing a team of any kind are very, very different. (Here, we're calling back to our cultural values of individualism and the conflation of individual performance with leadership.) An Artisan will be miserable with their increased meetings, the reporting relationships, monitoring dashboards... pretty much everything but their higher paychecks. A true Artisan will often find themselves willing to trade higher pay for the enjoyment of getting to do the craft and its associated processes that they excel in. Maker time vs manager time isn't something Artisans enjoy balancing—they *want* maker time.

Going back to our sayings from earlier, it is not necessarily that an Artisan will have a very low level of competence to manage people, but it will drain their energy and be unfulfilling.

One of the most flagrant offenders of promoting Artisans to roles begging for Seconds is higher education. Academics are by design engineered to be Artisans. They pass through a successive narrowing of their disciplinary focus until, in their Ph.D. programs, their doctoral dissertation is so narrow and deep that it would be irrelevant to 99 percent of the population. Academics who get teaching faculty positions are expected to teach courses and produce research in their niche of specialization. But there's a catch. Someone has to oversee the administrative duties of an academic department. Very few academics have any formal training in practical administration, and most academics do not want the "department chair" role. This is so much the case that academics typically sign up for a three-year term as department chair (at most). The chair role is often seen as interfering with their "real work" and potentially holding back advancements in their career.

If you've ever had the misfortune of being led at work by an Artisan whose niche brilliance was mistaken for administrative acumen, you know how dreadful it can be.

Seconds differ from Artisans in that they are happy to oversee processes and the people attached to them. Seconds will also readily learn new things outside of their prior focus areas to make the processes and people who report to them efficient and effective.

Artisans have a hugely important place in most organizations, including businesses—but they need Seconds around in order to stay focused on the work they have energy and high competence for.

How to Find and Live with a First in Command

We can see Seconds wanting to use this stuff to point the finger at anyone filling a First in Command role and saying, "You need to understand that you're messing this up—you're messing *us* up!" But it'll probably be a top three thing to remember from this book that we as Seconds are responsible for knowing who we are and saying "no" when we're asked to be people that we're not. If we haven't owned that and had generous conversations with our leaders about it, then we haven't even done our part yet and need to have a heap of grace for them.

Part of owning who we are for ourselves is choosing what team to join and, by proxy, who our First in Command will be.

It's actually not that hard to find a First in Command to join up with. The hard part is finding someone that really fits *you*.

As a Second, you possess the power to turn almost anyone, including yourself, into the person sitting in the First in Command role. That power means you can easily turn someone who has no business leading others into the person who is in charge of the organization you're now helping stay running.

There's a huge difference in people who are in a First in Command role and people who are naturally a 1iC or possess those visionary or strategist traits. The more Seconds lean into their natural talents, the more pressure they'll put on the person in the First in Command role. For instance, if the person in that First in Command role isn't as skilled in their role as a 2iC is in theirs, the 2iC won't just outperform them, they'll quickly come to see them as incompetent or frauds.

This isn't strictly an "experience" or "skills" thing. It has a lot to do with understanding what positions give you energy as a Second, and maintaining the ability to live in those places as much as you can. That means knowing those same things about your First in Command and letting them live in their own area of impact and energy. Whether you're taking on a Second in Command role *or* a Right Hand or manager role, you need to establish a mutual respect with your leader that sounds like, "Wow, you're a natural at that and you really enjoy it, and I *do not*—let's divide and conquer." This is typically easier if you can find a 1iC to pair up with since they tend to have a baseline set of traits that make them great partners for Seconds, both 2s and 2iCs.

If you've decided that you want to be First in Command, you should understand that it almost never works to find someone with a 1iC identity to join and lead the visioning for your idea. With rare exception, that's not how 1iCs naturally work. If you want to pair up with a natural 1iC, you'll most likely have to find someone who either wants to start their own thing, or is already stuck and looking for you to join their thing.

This is another reason it's so incredibly important to have a good understanding of yourself and the lanes you want to stay in—a 1iC who needs help will see their organization as this already beautiful boat that simply has some holes that need plugging... and to them, it looks like you have 100 fingers.

The more specific you get on the type of organization you want to be in, the better. Keep this in mind: if you're willing to go to where the job is and you're not talking about something niche, there are infinitely more of that type of company and positions available within them than there are Seconds in the world. If you decide you want to be the Second in Command of a record label that specializes in '20s style remixes of dubstep records, sure, you might have a tough time—but anything already more popular than that and you're probably good to go. There's already a group out there that needs your skills.

The following is an excerpt from an interview with Wil Reynolds, founder and current CEO of Seer Interactive. At the time of this interview, the Second in Command of Seer Interactive is named Crystal. This interview was conducted by Nathan Young.

Nathan Young: Just in general, where do you get your energy from?

Wil Reynolds: Building new things, I like to build new things. I like looking for places where our industry has accepted a status quo and finding another way to be like, "Why has everybody accepted this?" I like to be able to talk to someone and say, "A plus B equals C, right?" And your client's like, "Yeah." And then you're like, "Why has our industry avoided that reality? It's all sitting there for us. Why have we not embraced that reality?" And then I start to try to—how can we take something that, when everybody looks at it, it just makes sense, but then nobody's really solved that problem?

Nathan Young: Where do you think Crystal gets her energy from?

Wil Reynolds: Ooh, I think she—you know, it's hard to speak for somebody, but it's out of refining the crazy. It's like she considers herself oftentimes to be a refiner. And she's like, "You've got eighty different things you want to do? My job is to take those eighty and figure out which ones are the ones we should do, not do, ask tough questions [like] who is this solving a problem for? Is this a thing you're just excited about? Have you talked to clients about this? You talked to clients who are willing to pay for it?" Blah, blah, blah. I think it's *that*: how do I ask the right questions to help all of our executives get better and smarter?

And, you know, Crystal's the kind of person that probably says the least in the room, and then when she finally speaks, it's like, "Oh, shit!" She's the kind of person that you could think was not overly engaged in a meeting, right? She's not paying attention or whatever ...and then she says something, and she heard everything that was said. She processed it, put it through the wringer, let it go out six years, three years, two years, thought about the leading indicators, brought it back and now just said five words and you're like, "OH DAMN! WHAT!? You figured it all out!" You know?

Keeping Ideas Alive, and Where They Go

As a Second, you're going to intuitively see all the to-dos that the next big idea needs. But as Seconds (and especially if you're a 2iC) we need to keep enthusiasm high. Most ideas don't have to go into place tomorrow morning, so we don't need to start project managing and dissecting ideas right away. Our job is to grab the idea, stay excited about it, and ask questions later.

Remember to buy into the abilities of your First in Command, whatever type of person they are, and celebrate their vision and new ideas first. You can dissect it all later.

When it's time to ask questions, let your First in Command know that all of your questions are not nitpicking, they're just getting on the same page—and they're your version of taking action. For all Seconds, the need for a plan seems to be very high, and being a high factfinder seems to be a table stakes ability for 2iCs. As Seconds, we're just trying to pull out all the little details that might leave us and our First in Command talking past each other.

There are several common areas and questions that leadership teams, and specifically First in Command/Second in Command teams have. The relationship has been very well documented by others, and we feel we'd better serve you by pointing at those things for now, so see the resources section (chapter 11) for further details.

CHAPTER 10

I'VE REALLY FOUND MYSELF! ...NOW WHAT?!?

FIRST: A LITTLE WARNING about all of this identity stuff and making your next career move.

Seconds seem to be people who like assessments. As Seconds, we like them too. We're interested in gaining the self-insight that certain assessments profess to give. Perhaps you've run the gamut of personal inventory assessments, and like us, there seem to be parts of you that are highlighted. But more of you seems to remain unexplained—the assessments don't seem to show most of you in a reflection in one glance; you only see slivers of what might be you.

Like us, you may have run through the alphabet soup of personality and leadership assessments: MBTI, DiSC, MMPI, NEO PI-R, 16PF, HEXACO, MVPI, CPI, FIRO-B.... The list goes on probably almost as long as this book. Each one may shed some light to help you recognize aspects of yourself. But you've probably come to three realizations: 1) there's a saturation point where you're not learning much more about yourself, 2) you're not really sure what to do with these different slivers of information, and 3) there's no one assessment that can come close to encapsulating your essence.

In addition to those problems, our society often gives us strategies of figuring out our identities through uniqueness. That's part of the implied assumptions of a lot of the assessments that exist: they're best used to see how you're unique, and by compiling enough components, enough assessment type descriptions, etc., you can pile all of them up into a combination of unique aspects that makes you a unique, whole person.

But that doesn't work. Adding up a bunch of ways that you can vary does not provide a satisfactory sense of who you are. It does not form a satisfactory identity.

Our work here is not necessarily different. Finding all of the ways you are supposedly unique and slicing that thinner and thinner won't leave you with a marble statue that you can gaze upon as the true you, assuming you could ever find all of the ways to slice at all.

People are a living phenomena greater than their assessable parts.

This phenomenon-of-us can be even more confusing when it comes to choosing a career. The predominant model of figuring out career fit is known as "trait and factor." Traits are the things that all of these assessments are attempting to measure about us. Factors are aspects of different career fields or workplaces. Trait and factor theory says that by matching individual worker traits with factors of certain career fields or workplaces, you can predict a happy and successful career.

Trait and factor theory has been heavily critiqued, because it fails as much as it succeeds in its predictions. Worker satisfaction is based on more than just matching discrete traits with factors. Many of us know this in our bones. We picked the major, career, or job that matched some facets that we knew about ourselves. And we were (or are) miserable. But it still dominates the cultural imagination of how we think we can ensure employment satisfaction.

We both have experienced the unpleasant limitations of attempting to make what we knew about ourselves a predicter of career satisfaction. This book comes out of our experiences, often fumbling forward in the dark, trying to learn about ourselves and our ideal work scenarios *based on what didn't work*.

Maybe you're there, too. You're piling up the things that you don't want in a job next to the things you've learned about yourself through job situations you did not like. But you are tired of learning that way.

Part of job dissatisfaction stems from the basic principle that there are no perfect jobs. People who say things like, "If you love what you do, you'll never work a day in your life" are feeding you a line. At some level, work is… well, work.

But part of the problem is that we tend to focus on individual aspects as the way to figure out that we are unique. And that strategy tends to create fuzzy pictures that cloud as much as illuminate. For every small facet you add up that feels clear, the strategy may distort the size or importance of that aspect and mask something else that's important about you from your view.

The work of writing set us down a path based on a hunch, and the learning along the way has paid off in both of our lives. We definitely understand ourselves and how we fit into a workplace system much better for this experience and having spent so much time thinking on these concepts for ourselves. Most importantly, and we've said this multiple times, we are now able to own *all* of the facets of who we are—the ones we covered in this book and the ones we didn't. We hope and believe that many of you can and will have a similar experience.

How We (Nathan and David) Are Second

Like many pivotal events in life, it is not possible to distill all the different ways that writing this book has impacted us. Most of the impacts that we can discern stem from the fact that being 2 or a 2iC is an identity—something that is primarily inborn. As such, it is something that can be nurtured and developed. Also, it is something portable that goes with you throughout all areas of your life. There's something comforting in that fact; we don't need to chase after a role to ratify our status as a 2/2iC. Instead, we *are* 2s/2iCs. It's our starting point. We bring it to whatever professional or personal role we inhabit.

We also noticed a sense of convergence. Imagine a bunch of dots that appear scattered on a two-dimensional rendering. It looks chaotic, like there's no connection. However, if you take the same points in a three-dimensional space, you can potentially rotate these formerly disparate points and find that they align. In writing this book, we've been able to find these lenses of 2/2iC that made our qualities and tendencies converge. And in this convergence, our energy has been able to shift from reconciling the apparent divergences to moving forward in a concerted direction. What once felt scattered and in need of constant translation and explanation can now be mobilized and strategically deployed.

This has brought us a sense of peace in and a certain "settledness" about how we relate to the world. We both found new professional roles in the process of working on this book. Both of our roles were showcased by the research, pointing to each of us being a 2 and a 2iC, respectively.

For Nathan, he had a name (2iC) that prompted him to look within a certain swath of opportunities. Funnily enough, he is now simply called "Second in Command" in his new company. For David, he realized that he could take a leadership role as a Second without having to stretch to fit all the trappings of a 2iC. He can focus on leading a unit in a larger structure, paying attention to building processes that require deep interpersonal work with a team. There's a quiet confidence that we can fit the challenges of these roles, because we understand what we *do not* need to be or to focus on.

This convergence has created a sense of foresight and a different way to navigate potential setbacks. We each have a greater ability to not fall into traps of false responsibility or to get fixated on areas of weakness. It's been great to be upfront about things we need to do our jobs well. We can build proactive systems to help us stay in our lanes and create support systems to bolster areas where we're not at our strongest.

Before writing this book, we both had a tendency to let problem areas pile up at work until it felt like the job was a horrible fit and leaving was inevitable. Every role can have features that make them not ideal, especially for someone wired as a 2/2iC. But armed with a convergent sense of ourselves as a 2 and a 2iC, we are able to identify and inhabit roles differently. We don't have to be perfect in a role, and a role doesn't have to be perfect for us to take it.

In hindsight, the pursuit of the perfect role has often been a hope that the role would help define who we are. At best, a role can refine—but not fundamentally define—who we are.

Each of us has become a bit more at peace with our wiring. We've become a bit more settled in the question of who we are *and* who we are not. It's just as liberating to not be burdened with false expectations and assumptions of ourselves as to understand the stuff we are made of. It helps us sort through life: what to pick up and put down; where to spend time, energy, and money; what growth looks like versus mere achievement... It's a sense of walking through the world more on purpose. With a focus that fuzzes out things that are best handled by others in our world.

Our Mission Statement

You know that saying, "Just the tip of the iceberg"? This isn't even that, but we have at least found and named the iceberg.

Setting aside our personal feelings as a 2 and 2iC ourselves, we feel like our roles as authors and researchers ask us to tackle these two jobs for you and the rest of the Second community overall:

1. Help Seconds, both 2s and 2iCs, understand who they are and how that's valuable, *and* that it's *their* responsibility to own that identity.
2. Point Seconds in the direction of resources and tools so they can take their own next steps.

That's what we're hoping to accomplish, with this book as a starting point.

Tactically, we feel like we'll do well at those two jobs through three primary methods:

1. Promote the identity of Seconds to communities and leaders of communities through speaking and writing. (Starting with *this* book, but also things like podcasting and talking directly to existing community leaders.)
2. Create partnerships with those building the tools Seconds need, so when people self-identify and ask for the next step, we can point them in the right direction and help cushion the landing with good introductions. (Things like EOS, Pinnacle, hiring and assessment groups, COO Alliance, EO, YPO, masterminds, etc.)
3. Create and run some H2B2 mastermind groups that support the person as the main focus, with some time spent on tactical career needs or resource connections, since we as Seconds all find that valuable.

We believe reminding the people who turn ideas into reality that they're just as responsible for filtering as they are for fulfilling will improve quality of life for Seconds and also improve the new things coming into the world.

The change we want to usher into the world is one of Seconds empowered with identity and purpose to live in their area of maximum impact.

CHAPTER 11

RESOURCES

Nathan

Hey, it's Nathan—live from me to you. (This is not live, and we both know it. I just wanted to say that.)

We've mentioned the resources section of the book a few times throughout the writing. So here's a few things that might be helpful.

H2B2 STUFF

Our Website: HowToBeSecond.com

As of this writing, our website is primarily a sign-up for our email list and mastermind groups. We expect it to become a "Hub" destination of sorts over time, with links out to other helpful things for Seconds—extra reading material from other authors, other communities, resources for finding a job, (mostly) uncut interviews that we have done and will do, white papers on new things we're digging into around How to Be Second... you know, good stuff.

Our Email List: We send out the How to be Second community email on a "per useful thing happening" basis, but never more than once a week. Usually on Tuesday or Wednesday. Sign up for the list. If you do and then realize you don't like it, tell us why.

Mastermind Groups: As of this writing, we have a waiting list available to join or help facilitate one of our mastermind groups. Details for those groups can be found on our website. We'd love to have you. ***howtobesecond.com/mastermind***

Assessment: David is spearheading the development of our own personality assessment to help guide you in the question of "Am I a Second? A 2 or 2iC?" As of this writing, we are beta testing that. Get in touch if you're up for being a tester. ***howtobeSecond.com/assessment***

Find Nathan on Linkedin: Currently at ***linkedin.com/in/nathan-s-young*** until URL structures get adjusted or whatever. I talk about Second stuff incessantly and do most of my networking there. Connect with me. Mention the book. Do it. /flex

Find David on Linkedin: Currently at ***linkedin.com/in/david-hartman-ph-d/*** David spends a little less time lurking on "the socials," but it's still a great place to connect with him.

Other social media: I've posted some stuff on my personal YouTube channel, but we currently have no plans to build this out; it's just not in our areas of energy. If you're all in on this stuff and would love to do some social media things for How to be Second out of an abundance of energy and the desire to be a raving fan, give us a shout! (Not as a solicitation, though.)

COMMUNITIES

These all exist at the time of this writing, but you know how communities like this work—they might disappear at any time. For the most current list of what we know is available, ping us or check out ***howtobesecond.com/communities***

The COO Alliance is run by Cameron Herold, and as the website says, it's "The World's Leading Community for the Second In Command." Cameron did an interview for our book and we follow and talk about his work a lot, so you should mention us if you go over there. We don't get any checks for referring you over there, but maybe if a few of you mention our names he'll send us something cool! ***COOAlliance.com***

The LIFT Integrator Community™ from Authentic Brand is for those who "are in the Integrator seat/have Integrator or 'Second in Command' accountabilities." I've attended a few of these myself and met some friends. I've also had the opportunity to meet Jennifer on a few occasions to chat with her about the community and she's always been fantastic. Again, no affiliation other than that. Mention us if you go. ***authenticbrand.com/lift-Integrator-community***

Female Integrator Mastermind (FIM) built by Kristie Clayton and her incredible team have done fantastic things, and all I see about this community is love. Kristie generously did an interview for the book and is quoted in it. Once again, just a lovely person doing a lovely thing. Mention us if you go. ***Integratormastermind.com***

Rocket Fuel University^{TM} is currently run by Mark Winters, who co-wrote the book *Rocket Fuel* and seems to be a helpful resource for people working in the Integrator role while using the EOS system in a business. I believe they maintain a community of sorts. I myself am an Integrator Masterclass graduate, though I admit to having mostly moved on from participation in the community. Mention us if you go, though! ***rocketfueluniversity.com/rocket-fuel-book***

If you have a community for Seconds, Second in Commands, or people who you think are this thing, and you'd love to be listed in our communities, get in touch!

OTHER PEOPLE'S CONTENT

If you're a Second In Command and hold the title of COO, VP Ops, President, etc., check out the Second in Command podcast from Cameron Herold.

We don't think that everyone Cameron interviews is a natural Second, which is actually helpful. It's interesting to hear about how people navigate the *role* without the identity, and it's fun to hear people who *are* 2s and 2iCs attempt to talk about their unique traits without any of the language that we're hoping this book finally provides. ***cooalliance. com/podcasts***